# *Wise and Witty* QUIPS & QUOTATIONS

*Compiled by*
**Bollimuntha Venkata Raman Rao**

**PUSTAK MAHAL®**

J-3/16 , Daryaganj, New Delhi-110002
☎ 23276539, 23272783, 23272784 • *Fax:* 011-23260518
*E-mail:* info@pustakmahal.com • *Website:* www.pustakmahal.com

*Sales Centre*

- 10-B, Netaji Subhash Marg, Daryaganj, New Delhi-110002
  ☎ 23268292, 23268293, 23279900 • *Fax:* 011-23280567
  *E-mail:* rapidexdelhi@indiatimes.com
- **Hind Pustak Bhawan**
  6686, Khari Baoli, Delhi-110006
  ☎ 23944314, 23911979

*Branches*

**Bengaluru:** ☎ 080-22234025 • *Telefax:* 080-22240209
*E-mail*: pustak@airtelmail.in • pustak@sancharnet.in
**Mumbai:** ☎ 022-22010941, 022-22053387
*E-mail*: rapidex@bom5.vsnl.net.in
**Patna:** ☎ 0612-3294193 • *Telefax:* 0612-2302719
*E-mail*: rapidexptn@rediffmail.com
**Hyderabad:** *Telefax:* 040-24737290
*E-mail*: pustakmahalhyd@yahoo.co.in

*This book was earlier published under the title*
**"The Book of Uncommon Quips & Quotations"**



ISBN 978-81-223-0840-2

**Edition: 2011**



*Printed at :* **Unique Colour Cartoon, Delhi**

# Preface

A book of witty and wise quotes can, at times, teach one much more in a few hours than a lifetime of bumbling around. Many a times, we come across witty quotes and sayings that are soon forgotten. It was these thoughts that prompted me to compile a book of the most witty and wise quotes and proverbs that I had come across.

The focus of this book, though, is more on animals, nature and man. Many quotes of the rich and famous stress the importance of compassion towards all our fellow creatures that inhabit the earth.

I sincerely hope that the words of wit and wisdom contained in this book will prompt readers to display more compassion towards all living beings.

The quotes have been culled from many different sources and my sincere thanks to all the previous compilers and authors.

**—Bollimuntha Venkata Ramana Rao**

# Contents

Animal Quotes and Quips ........ 7
Dog Days ........ 21
Cat Wisdom ........ 29
Divine Nature ........ 36
The Magic of Flowers ........ 49
Cow Tales ........ 55
Elephant Talk ........ 56
Horse Sense ........ 57
Mouse Moves ........ 60
Porky Pig ........ 61
The Question of Beauty ........ 62
The Call of Birds ........ 71
Beautiful Butterflies ........ 77
Season's Greetings ........ 78
Charming Smiles ........ 82
The Essence of Happiness ........ 86
Musical Notes ........ 94
Man and Animal ........ 100
Feminine Talk ........ 108
Man Talk, Woman Talk ........ 110
Life Speak ........ 111
Garden Wisdom ........ 116
Tree Tales ........ 119
Ant Antics ........ 121
Man & Miscellany ........ 122

# Animal Quotes and Quips

Animals are my friends, and I don't eat my friends.

**—George Bernard Shaw**

❍❖❍

I am fond of pigs. Dogs look up to us. Cats look down. Pigs treat us as equals.

**—Winston Churchill**

❍❖❍

Behold the turtle. He makes progress only when he sticks his neck out.

**—James Bryant Conant**

❍❖❍

When you see a snake, you just kill it; don't appoint a committee on snakes.

**—Chris Noble**

❍❖❍

A closed mouth catches no flies.

**—Miguel de Cervantes**

❍❖❍

Wooing the press is an exercise roughly akin to picnicking with a tiger. You might enjoy the meal, but the tiger always eats last.

**—Maureen Dowd**

❍❖❍

Grasshopper always wrong in argument with chicken.

**—Chinese Proverb**

❍❖❍

If you are losing a tug of war with a tiger, give him the rope before he gets to your arm. You can always buy a new rope.

**—Max Gunther**

❍❖❍

Ever considered what pets must think of us? I mean, here we come back from a grocery store with the most amazing haul – chicken, pork, half a cow. They must think we're the greatest hunters on earth!

**—Anne Tyler**

❍❖❍

When rats leave a sinking ship, where exactly do they think they're going?

**—Douglas Gauck**

❍❖❍

A beaver does not, as legend would have it, know which direction the tree will fall when he cuts it, but counts on alacrity to make up for the lack of engineering expertise.

**—Ann Zwinger**

❍❖❍

We call them dumb animals, and so they are, for they cannot tell us how they feel, but they do not suffer less because they have no words.

**—Anna Sewell**

❍❖❍

The time will come when public opinion will no longer tolerate amusements based on the mistreatment and killing of animals. The time will come, but when?

**—Albert Schweitzer**

❍❖❍

I once decided not to date a guy because he wasn't excited to meet my dog. I mean – this was like not wanting to meet my mother.

**—Bonnie Schacter**

❍❖❍

We hope that, when the insects take over the world, they will remember with gratitude how we took them along on our picnics.

**—Bill Vaughan**

We are part of the earth and it is part of us. The perfumed flowers are our sisters; the deer, the horse, the great eagle, these are our brothers. All things are connected like the blood which unites one's family.

**—Chief Seattle**

❍❖❍

Before us the creatures fall – some diminished, some wiped completely from the face of the Creator's canvas. Before us is the trashed gallery of earth's Maker.

**—Calvin DeWitt**

❍❖❍

*If, strolling forth, a beast you view*
*Whose hide with spots is peppered,*
*As soon as it has leapt on you*
*You'll know it is a leopard.*

**—Carolyn Wells**

❍❖❍

*The horse and mule live thirty years*
*And never know of wine and beers.*
*The goat and sheep at twenty die*
*Without a taste of scotch or rye.*
*The cow drinks water by the ton*
*And at eighteen is mostly done.*
*The dog at fifteen cashes in*
*Without the aid of rum or gin.*
*The modest, sober, bone-dry hen*
*Lays eggs and eggs and dies at ten.*

**—Charles Duffy**

❍❖❍

It's not much of a tail, but I'm sort-of attached to it.

**—Eyore**

❍❖❍

The quizzical expression of the monkey at the zoo comes from his wondering whether he is his brother's keeper, or his keeper's brother.

**—Evan Esar**

I fear animals regard man as a creature of their own kind, which has in a highly dangerous fashion lost its healthy animal reason – as the mad animal, as the laughing animal, as the weeping animal, as the unhappy animal.

**—Friedrich Nietzsche**

❍❖❍

The fly sat upon the axle-tree of the chariot wheel and said, 'What a dust do I raise!'

**—Francis Bacon**

❍❖❍

Animals generally return the love you lavish on them by a swift bite in passing – not unlike friends and wives.

**—Gerald Durrell**

❍❖❍

The world has different owners at sunrise... Even your own garden does not belong to you. Rabbits and blackbirds have the lawns; a tortoise-shell cat, who never appears in daytime, patrols the brick walls, and a golden-tailed pheasant glints his way through the iris spears.

**—Anne Morrow Lindbergh**

❍❖❍

Animals are such agreeable friends, they ask no questions, they pass no criticisms.

**—George Eliot**

❍❖❍

Animals are in possession of themselves; their soul is in possession of their body. But they have no right to their life, because they do not will it.

**—Georg Hegel**

❍❖❍

Whoever said you can't buy happiness forgot little puppies.

**—Gene Hill**

❍❖❍

The whale only gets harpooned when he spouts.

**—Henry Lea Hillman**

❍❖❍

*Whales play in an amniotic paradise.*
*Their light minds shaped by buoyancy,*
*Unrestricted by gravity,*
*Somersaulting.*
*Like angels, or birds;*
*Like our own lives, in the womb.*

**—Heathcote Williams**

❍❖❍

He who is cruel to animals becomes hard also in his dealings with men. We can judge the heart of a man by his treatment of animals.

**—Immanuel Kant**

❍❖❍

Animals, in their generation, are wiser than the sons of men; but their wisdom is confined to a few particulars, and lies in a very narrow compass.

**—Joseph Addison**

❍❖❍

*Always be kind to animals,*
*Morning, noon and night:*
*For animals have feelings too,*
*And furthermore, they bite.*

**—John Gardner**

❍❖❍

I believe in my heart that faith in Jesus Christ can and will lead us beyond an exclusive concern for the well-being of other human beings to the broader concern for the well-being of the birds in our backyards, the fish in our rivers, and every living creature on the face of the earth.

**—John Wesley**

❍❖❍

They [cats] smell, they snarl and they scratch; they have a singular aptitude for shredding rugs, drapes and upholstery; they're sneaky, selfish and not at all smart; they are disloyal, condescending and totally useless in any rodent-free environment.

**—Jean Michel Chapereau**

Always behave like a duck – keep calm and unruffled on the surface but paddle like the devil underneath.

**—Jacob Braude**

❍❖❍

I had a linguistics professor who said that it's man's ability to use language that makes him the dominant species on the planet. That may be. But I think there's one other thing that separates us from animals – we aren't afraid of vacuum cleaners.

**—Jeff Stilson**

❍❖❍

The cockroach and the bird were both here long before we were. Both could get along very well without us, although it is perhaps significant that of the two the cockroach would miss us more.

**—Joseph Wood Krutch**

❍❖❍

To me, cruelty is the worst of human sins. Once we accept that a living creature has feelings and suffers pain, then by knowingly and deliberately inflicting suffering on that creature, we are guilty, whether it be human or animal.

**—Jane Goodall**

❍❖❍

The tendency to cruelty should be watched in children and if they incline to any such cruelty, they should be taught the contrary usage. For the custom of tormenting and killing other animals will, by degrees, harden their hearts even towards man. Children should, from the beginning, be brought up in an abhorrence of killing or tormenting living beings.

**—John Locke**

❍❖❍

We must plant the sea and herd its animals – using the sea as farmers instead of hunters. That is what civilisation is all about – farming replacing hunting.

**—Jacques Cousteau**

Mosquitoes remind us that we are not as high up on the food chain as we think.

**—Tom Wilson**

❍❖❍

Animals give me more pleasure through the viewfinder of a camera than they ever did in the crosshairs of a gun sight. And after I've finished "shooting", my unharmed victims are still around for others to enjoy. I have developed a deep respect for animals. I consider them fellow living creatures with certain rights that should not be violated any more than those of humans.

**—Jimmy Stewart**

❍❖❍

To the ass, or the sow, their own offspring appear the fairest in creation.

**—Latin Proverb**

❍❖❍

No matter how little money and how few possessions you own, having a dog makes you rich.

**—Louis Sabin**

❍❖❍

An animal's eyes have the power to speak a great language.

**—Martin Buber**

❍❖❍

Any glimpse into the life of an animal quickens our own and makes it so much the larger and better in every way.

**—John Muir**

❍❖❍

Remember that gophers also need to make a living; preferably in somebody else's garden. When you can't fight on and drop to die, you're just a big tasty feast for the crows, ants, buzzards and flies.

Your dog will always shit near your favourite garden seat. Your wet and smelly dog always likes to cosy up real close while you're weeding. If dogs and cats craved raw vegetables, they would have never become pets.

**—Michael P Garofalo**

❍❖❍

Mankind's true moral test, its fundamental test, consists of its attitude towards those who are at its mercy: animals. And in this respect mankind has suffered a fundamental debacle, a debacle so fundamental that all others stem from it.

**—Milan Kundera**

❍❖❍

Confront a child, a puppy, and a kitten with a sudden danger; the child will turn instinctively for more assistance, the puppy will grovel in abject submission, the kitten will brace its tiny body for a frantic resistance.

**—Hector Hugh Munro**

❍❖❍

We think caged birds sing, when indeed they cry.

**—John Webster**

❍❖❍

In a few generations more, there will probably be no room at all allowed for animals on the earth: no need of them, no toleration of them. An immense agony will have then ceased, but with it there will also have passed away the last smile of the world's youth.

**—Quida**

❍❖❍

Humans are the only animals that have children on purpose with the exception of guppies – who like to eat theirs.

**—PJ Rourke**

❍❖❍

There is the little matter of disposal of droppings in which the cat is far ahead of its rivals. The dog is somehow thrilled by what he or any of his friends have produced, hates to leave it, adores smelling it, and sometimes eats it… The cat covers it up if he can…

**—Paul Gallico**

❍❖❍

The obligations of law and equity reach only to mankind; but kindness and beneficence should be extended to the creatures of every species, and these will flow from the breast of a true man, as streams that issue from the living fountain.

**—Plutarch**

I identify most strongly with the turtle: I patiently plod along till I reach my destination — and occasionally I stick out my neck.

**—Paulette Peltan**

❍❖❍

The gods created certain kinds of beings to replenish our bodies... they are the trees, the plants and the seeds.

**—Plato**

❍❖❍

I got the impression that instead of going out to shoot birds, I should go out and shoot the kids who shoot birds.

**—Paul Watson**

❍❖❍

I've actually gone to the zoo and had monkeys shout to me from their cages – I'm in here when you're walking around like that?

**—Robin Williams**

❍❖❍

*My heart's in the highlands, my heart is not here;*
*My heart's in the highlands a-chasing the deer.*

**—Robert Burns**

❍❖❍

What the caterpillar calls the end of the world, the master calls a butterfly.

**—Richard Bach**

❍❖❍

*The woods were made for the hunters of dreams,*
*The brooks for the fishers of song;*
*To the hunters who hunt for the gun-less game,*
*The streams and the woods belong.*

**—Sam Walter Foss**

❍❖❍

- A hen is only an egg's way of making another egg.
- All animals but man know that the principle business of life is to enjoy it – and they do enjoy it as much as man and circumstances will allow it.

**—Samuel Butler**

❍❖❍

A fly, sir, may sting a stately horse and make him wince; but one is but an insect, and the other is a horse still.

**—Samuel Johnson**

❍❖❍

Things that upset a terrier may pass virtually unnoticed by a Great Dane.

**—Smiley Blanton**

❍❖❍

If you have men who will exclude any of God's creatures from the shelter of compassion and pity, you will have men who will deal likewise with their fellow men.

**—St. Francis of Assisi**

The elephant, not only the largest, but the most intelligent of animals, provides us with an excellent example. It is faithful and tenderly loving to the female of its choice, mating only every third year and then for no more than five days, and so secretly as never to be seen, until, on the sixth day, it appears and goes at once to wash its whole body in the river, unwilling to return to the herd until thus purified. Such good and modest habits are an example to husband and wife.

**—St. Francis de Sales**

Method is more important than strength... By dropping golden beads near a snake, a crow once managed to have a passer-by kill the snake for the beads.

**—Siddha Nagarjuna**

Imagine if birds were tickled by feathers. You'd see a flock of birds come by, laughing hysterically!

**—Steven Wright**

Did you ever notice, when you blow in a dog's face he gets mad at you? But when you take him in a car he sticks his head out of the window.

**—Steve Bluestone**

The best thing about animals is they don't talk much.

**—Thornton Wilder**

❍❖❍

Animals are considered as property only. To destroy or to abuse them, from malice to the proprietor, or with an intention injurious to his interest in them, is criminal. But the animals themselves are without protection. The law regards them not substantively. They have NO RIGHTS!

**—Shirley Lord**

❍❖❍

Once it [cat] has given its love, what absolute confidence, what fidelity of affection! It will make itself the companion of your hours of work, of loneliness, or of sadness. It will lie the whole evening on your knee, purring and happy in your society, and leaving the company of creatures of its own society to be with you.

**—Theophile Gautier**

❍❖❍

I am more afraid of an army of a hundred sheep led by a lion than an army of a hundred lions led by a sheep.

**—Talleyrand**

❍❖❍

I do not see any reason why animals should be slaughtered to serve as human diet when there are so many substitutes. After all, man can live without meat.

**—Tenzing Gyatso**

❍❖❍

If you can dream it, you can do it. Always remember this whole thing was started by a mouse.

**—Walt Disney**

❍❖❍

If happiness truly consisted in physical ease and freedom from care, the happiest individual would not be either a man or a woman, but an American cow.

**—William Lyon Phelps**

❍❖❍

From the oyster to the eagle, from the swine to the tiger, all animals are to be found in men and each of them exists in some man, sometimes several at the time. Animals are nothing but the portrayal of our virtues and vices made manifest to our eyes, the visible reflections of our souls. God displays them to us to give us food for thought.

**—Victor Hugo**

❍❖❍

- I envy animals for two things – their ignorance of evil to come, and their ignorance of what is said about them.
- Animals have these advantages over man: they never hear the clock strike, they die without any idea of death, they have no theologians to instruct them, their last moments are not disturbed by unwelcome and unpleasant ceremonies, their funerals cost them nothing, and no one starts lawsuits over their wills.

**—Voltaire**

❍❖❍

*I talk to him [dog] when I'm lonesome like,*
*and I'm sure he understands.*
*When he looks at me so attentively,*
*and gently licks my hands;*
*Then he rubs his nose on my tailored clothes,*
*but I never say naught there at.*
*For the good Lord knows I can buy more clothes,*
*but never a friend like that.*

**—W Dayton Wedgefarth**

❍❖❍

- They [dog] do not sweat and whine about their condition, they do not lie awake in the dark and weep for their sins, they do not make me sick discussing their duty to God, not one is dissatisfied, not one is demented with the mania of owning things, not one kneels to another, nor to his kind that lived thousands of years ago.
- *O to be self-balanced for contingencies!*
  *O to confront night, storms, hunger, ridicule,*
  *Accidents, rebuffs as trees and animals do!*

**—Walt Whitman**

- Mary had a little lamb and the doctor fainted.
- Just when you think you've won the rat race along come faster rats.
- Even the lion has to defend himself against flies.
- Swallow a toad in the morning and you will encounter nothing more disgusting the rest of the day.
- If you think that something small cannot make a difference – try going to sleep with a mosquito in the room.
- When counting, try not to mix chickens with blessings.
- Even if you've been fishing for three hours and haven't gotten anything except poison-ivy and sunburn, you're still better off than the worm.
- If you hear the sound of hoof beats, don't look for zebra!
- When you see a snake, never mind where he came from.
- Fish are supposed to be brain food, and yet people eat it on Friday and then do the silliest things over the weekend.
- When God made the animals, He had us in mind...<br>They would need people with hearts warm and kind.<br>And we would need something to fill up the space<br>That He left in our hearts called 'The Animal Place'.<br>So hug them and love them.
- He is your friend, your partner, your defender, your dog. You are his life, his love, his leader. He will be yours, faithful and true, to the last beat of his heart. You owe it to him to be worthy of such devotion.
- I think animal testing is a terrible idea; they get all nervous and give the wrong answers.
- A dog thinks: 'Hey, these people I live with feed me, love me, provide me with a nice, warm, dry house, pet me, and take good care of me... They must be Gods!'

  A cat thinks: 'Hey, these people I live with feed me, love me, provide me with a nice, warm, dry house, pet me, and take good care of me... I must be God!'

**—Anonymous**

If people were superior to animals, they'd take better care of the world.

**—Winnie the Pooh**

❍❖❍

*The cattle are grazing,*
*Their heads never raising;*
*There are forty feeding like one!*

**—William Wordsworth**

❍❖❍

When we kill animals to eat them, they end up killing us because their flesh, which contains cholesterol and saturated fat, was never intended for human beings, who are natural herbivores.

**—William Clifford Roberts**

# Dog Days

DOG, noun: A subsidiary Deity designed to catch the overflow and surplus of the world's worship... His master works for the means wherewith to purchase the idle wag of the Solomonic tail, seasoned with a look of tolerant recognition.

**—Ambrose Bierce**

❍❖❍

The average dog is a nicer person than the average person.

**—Andrew A Rooney**

❍❖❍

Our dogs will love and admire the meanest of us, and feed our colossal vanity with their uncritical homage.

**—Agnes Repplier**

❍❖❍

History is more full of examples of the fidelity of dogs than of friends.

**—Alexander Pope**

❍❖❍

To his dog, every man is King; hence the constant popularity of dogs.

**—Aldous Huxley**

❍❖❍

Old dogs, like old shoes, are comfortable. They might be a bit out of shape and a little worn around the edges, but they fit well.

**—Bonnie Wilcox**

❍❖❍

Like a dog, he hunts in dreams.

**—Alfred Tennyson**

❍❖❍

I have caught more ills from people sneezing over me and giving me virus infections than from kissing dogs.

**—Barbara Woodhouse**

❍❖❍

A dog is the only thing on earth that loves you more than he loves himself.

**—Josh Billings**

❍❖❍

When a dog bites a man that is not news, but when a man bites a dog that is news.

**—Charles Dana Anderson**

❍❖❍

Bulldogs are adorable, with faces like toads that have been sat on.

**—Colette**

❍❖❍

No one appreciates the very special genius of your conversation as the dog does.

**—Christopher Morley**

❍❖❍

If you get to thinking you're a person of some influence, try orderin' somebody else's dog around.

**—Cowboy Wisdom**

❍❖❍

My dog is half pit bull, half poodle. Not much of a watchdog, but a vicious gossip!

**—Craig Shoemaker**

❍❖❍

But I have always liked bird dogs rather than kennel-fed dogs myself – you know, one that will get out and hunt for food rather than sit on his fanny and yell.

**—Charles E Wilson**

Happiness to a dog is what lies on the other side of a door.

**—Charleton**

❍❖❍

A dog is not considered a good dog because he is a good barker. A man is not considered a good man because he is a good talker.

**—Chuang Tzu**

❍❖❍

Dogs have more love than integrity. They've been true to us, yes, but they haven't been true to themselves.

**—Clarence Day**

❍❖❍

- Dogs feel very strongly that they should always go with you in the car, in case the need should arise for them to bark violently at nothing, right in your ear.
- You can say any fool thing to a dog, and the dog will give you this look that says, 'My God, you're RIGHT! I NEVER would've thought of that!'

**—Dave Barry**

❍❖❍

What counts is not necessarily the size of the dog in the fight; it's the size of the fight in the dog.

**—Dwight Eisenhower**

❍❖❍

They say a reasonable amount of fleas is good for a dog – keeps him from brooding over being a dog.

**—Edward Westcott**

❍❖❍

In order to really enjoy a dog, one doesn't merely try to train him to be semi-human. The point of it is to open oneself to the possibility of becoming partly a dog.

**—Edward Hoagland**

❍❖❍

If you are a dog and your owner suggests that you wear a sweater… suggest that he wear a tail.

**—Fran Lebowitz**

❍❖❍

You learn in this business: If you want a friend, get a dog.

**—Carl Icahn**

❍❖❍

What kind of life a dog… acquires. I have sometimes tried to imagine by kneeling or lying full length on the ground and looking up. The world then becomes strangely incomplete; one sees little but legs.

**—EV Lucas**

❍❖❍

I think dogs are the most amazing creatures; they give unconditional love. For me they are the role model for being alive.

**—Gilda Radner**

❍❖❍

I like dogs better [than people]. They give you unconditional love. They either lick your face or bite you, but you always know where they're coming from. With people, you never know which ones will bite. The difference between dogs and men is that you know where dogs sleep at night.

**—Greg Louganis**

❍❖❍

I think we are drawn to dogs because they are the uninhibited creatures we might be if we weren't certain we knew better.

**—George Bird Evans**

❍❖❍

The dog was created specially for children. He is the god of frolic.

**—Henry Ward Beecher**

❍❖❍

Money will buy you a pretty good dog, but it won't buy the wag of his tail.

**—Henry Wheeler Shaw**

❍❖❍

The biggest dog has been a pup.

**—Joaquin Miller**

❍❖❍

Never stand between a dog and the hydrant.

**—John Peers**

❍❖❍

In my day, we didn't have dogs or cats. All I had was Silver Beauty, my beloved paper clip.

**—Jennifer Hart**

❍❖❍

Dogs come when they're called. Cats take a message and get back to you.

**—Mary Fly**

❍❖❍

Better not take a dog on the space shuttle, because if he sticks his head out when you're coming home his face might burn up.

**—Jack Handy**

❍❖❍

I have always thought of a dog lover as a dog that was in love with another dog.

**—James Thurber**

❍❖❍

My dog is usually pleased with what I do, because she is not infected with the concept of what I "should" be doing.

**—Lonzo Idolswine**

❍❖❍

Dogs laugh, but they laugh with their tails. What puts man in a higher state of evolution is that he has got his laugh on the right end.

**—Max Eastman**

❍❖❍

Dogs are getting bigger, according to a leading dog manufacturer.

**—Leo Rosten**

❍❖❍

Life is like a dog sled team. If you ain't the lead dog, the scenery never changes.

**—Lewis Grizzard**

❍❖❍

The dog is a 'Yes' animal. Very popular with people who can't afford a 'Yes' man.

**—Robertson Davies**

❍❖❍

Dogs are our link to paradise. They don't know evil or jealousy or discontent. To sit with a dog on a hillside on a glorious afternoon is to be back in Eden, where doing nothing was not boring – it was peace.

**—Milan Kundera**

❍❖❍

Every dog must have his day.

**—Jonathan Swift**

❍❖❍

A dog is a dog, a bird is a bird, and a cat is a person.

**—Mugsy Peabody**

❍❖❍

- The more I know about people, the better I like my dog.
- The dog is a gentleman; I hope to go to his heaven, not man's.
- If you take a dog which is starving and feed him and make him prosperous, that dog will not bite you. This is the primary difference between a dog and a man.

**—Mark Twain**

❍❖❍

- A dog's best friend is his illiteracy.
- A door is what a dog is perpetually on the wrong side of.
- *The dog is man's best friend,*
  *He has a tail on one end.*
  *Up in front he has teeth,*
  *And four legs underneath.*

**—Ogden Nash**

❍❖❍

- A dog teaches a boy fidelity, perseverance, and to turn around three times before lying down.
- Dogs have given us their absolute all. We are the centre of their universe. We are the focus of their love, faith and trust. They serve us in return for scraps. It is without a doubt the best deal man has ever made.

**—Roger Caras**

❍❖❍

Many dogs will give a greeting grin much like a human smile.

**—Richard A Walters**

❍❖❍

*His name is not Wild Dog any more,*
*but the First Friend.*
*Because he will be our friend,*
*for always and always and always.*

**—Rudyard Kipling**

❍❖❍

*The dog barks backward without getting up*
*So I can remember when he was a pup.*

**—Robert Frost**

❍❖❍

I would rather see the portrait of a dog that I know, than all the allegorical paintings they can show me in the world.

**—Samuel Johnson**

❍❖❍

The greatest pleasure of a dog is that you may make a fool of yourself with him and not only will he not scold you, but he will make a fool of himself too.

**—Samuel Butler**

❍❖❍

Breed not a savage dog, nor permit a loose stairway.

**—Talmud**

❍❖❍

I put contact lenses in my dog's eyes. They had little pictures of cats on them. Then I took one out and he ran around in circles.

**—Steven Wright**

❍❖❍

Did you ever walk into a room and forget why you walked in? I think that is how dogs spend their lives.

**—Sue Murphy**

❍❖❍

A barking dog is often more useful than a sleeping lion.

**—Washington Irving**

In the beginning God created man, but seeing him so feeble, he gave him the dog.

**—Toussenel**

❍❖❍

I've been on so many blind dates, I should get a free dog.

**—Wendy Liebman**

❍❖❍

If a dog will not come to you after having looked you in the face, you should go home and examine your conscience.

**—Woodrow Wilson**

❍❖❍

- I love a dog. He does nothing for political reasons.
- No man can be condemned for owning a dog. As long as he has a dog, he has a friend; and the poorer he gets, the better friend he has.

**—Will Rogers**

Of all the things I miss from veterinary practice, puppy breath is one of the most fond memories!

**—Dr Tom Cat**

❍❖❍

- When a dog wags her tail and barks at the same time, how do you know which end to believe?
- A dog can express more with his tail in minutes than his owner can express with his tongue in hours.
- Every boy who has a dog should also have a mother, so the dog can be fed regularly.
- One dog barks at something, the rest bark at him.
- In dog years, I'm dead.
- To err is human, to forgive, canine.
- If your dog doesn't like someone, you probably shouldn't either.
- When you feel dog-tired at night, it may be because you've growled all day long.

**—Anonymous**

# Cat Wisdom

CAT, noun: A soft, indestructible automaton provided by nature to be kicked when things go wrong in the domestic circle.

**—Ambrose Pierce**

Cats are smarter than dogs. You cannot get eight cats to pull a sled through snow.

**—Jeff Valdez**

No matter how much cats fight, there always seems to be plenty of kittens.

**—Abraham Lincoln**

There are two means of refuge from the miseries of life: music and cats.

**—Albert Schweitzer**

After scolding one's cat, one looks into its face and is seized by the ugly suspicion that it understood every word. And has filed it for reference.

**—Charlotte Gray**

A cat isn't fussy – just so long as you remember he likes his milk in the shallow, rose-patterned saucer and his fish on the blue plate. From which he will take it, and eat it off the floor.

**—Arthur Bridges**

Curiosity is the very basis of education and if you tell me that curiosity killed the cat, I say only the cat died nobly.

**—Arnold Edinborough**

❍❖❍

We all have our 'good old days' tucked away inside our hearts, and we return to them in daydreams like cats to favourite armchairs.

**—Brian Carter**

❍❖❍

A cat is there when you call her – if she doesn't have something better to do.

**—Bill Adler**

❍❖❍

At night he [the cat] sleeps sprawled at the foot of my bed, where he snores reassuringly until about five in the morning. That's when he gets cuddly: with white paw – claws retracted – he pats my face until I open my eyes. The fact that I then throw him out and slam the door in his face doesn't bother him.

**—Cathryn Jakobson**

❍❖❍

A cat playing around is normal behaviour; a cat playing on your head at four o'clock in the morning is not appropriate behaviour from a human point of view.

**—Dale Olm**

❍❖❍

People who hate cats will come back as mice in their next life.

**—Faith Resnick**

❍❖❍

God created domestic cats so that men might touch tigers.

**—DAN**

❍❖❍

The cat has too much spirit to have no heart.

**—Ernest Menaul**

❍❖❍

Which is more beautiful – feline movement or feline stillness?

**—Elizabeth Hamilton**

❍❖❍

We have a theory that cats are planning to take over the world; just try to look them straight in the eye... yup, they're hiding something!

**—Dog Fancy**

❍❖❍

- One cat just leads to another.
- A cat has absolute emotional honesty; human beings for one reason or another may hide their feelings, but a cat does not.

**—Ernest Hemingway**

❍❖❍

Cats are living adornments.

**—Edwin Lent**

❍❖❍

With the qualities of cleanliness, affection, patience, dignity, and courage that cats have, how many of us, I ask you, would be capable of becoming cats?

**—Fernand Mery**

❍❖❍

Everything I know I learned from my cat: When you're hungry, eat. When you're tired, nap in a sunbeam. When you go to the vet's, pee on your owner.

**—Gary Smith**

❍❖❍

Cats are intended to teach us that not everything in nature has a purpose.

**—Garrison Keillor**

❍❖❍

A cat sneezing is a good omen for everyone who hears it.

**—Italian Superstition**

❍❖❍

- Cats seem to go on the principle that it never does any harm to ask for what you want.
- Cats are rather delicate creatures and they are subject to a good many ailments, but I never heard of one who suffered from insomnia.

**—Joseph Wood Crutch**

❍❖❍

I have noticed that what cats most appreciate in a human being is not the ability to produce food, which they take for granted – but his or her entertainment value.

**—Geoffrey Household**

❍❖❍

You cannot look at a sleeping cat and feel tense.

**—Jane Pauley**

❍❖❍

Cats are the ultimate narcissists. You can tell this because of all the time they spend on personal grooming. Dogs aren't like this. A dog's idea of personal grooming is to roll on a dead fish.

**—James Gorman**

❍❖❍

To some blind souls all cats are much alike. To a cat lover every cat from the beginning of time has been utterly and amazingly unique.

**—Jenny de Vries**

❍❖❍

- When you are looking a cat acts like a princess, but the minute she thinks you are not looking, a cat acts like a fool.
- The reason cats climb is so that they can look down on almost every other animal... it's also the reason they hate birds.

**—KC Buffington**

❍❖❍

You may own a cat, but cannot govern one.

**—Kate Sanborn**

❍❖❍

The smallest feline is a masterpiece.

**—Leonardo da Vinci**

❍❖❍

Two cats can live as cheaply as one, and their owner has twice as much fun.

**—Lloyd Alexander**

❍❖❍

Never try to out-stubborn a cat.

**—Lazarus Long**

❍❖❍

Cats are glorious creatures – who must on no accounts be underestimated... Their eyes are fathomless depths of cat-world mysteries.

**—Lesley Anne Ivory**

❍❖❍

He [the cat] liked to peep into the refrigerator and risk having his head shut in by the closing door. He also climbed to the top of the stove, discontinuing the practice after he singed his tail.

**—Lloyd Alexander**

❍❖❍

- Most cats, when they are out want to be in, and vice versa, and often simultaneously.
- Cat people are different, to the extent that they generally are not conformists. How could they be, with a cat running their lives?

**—Louis J Camuti**

❍❖❍

Cats are notoriously sore losers. Coming in second best, especially to someone as poorly coordinated as a human being, grates their sensibility.

**—Stephen Baker**

❍❖❍

When I play with my cat, who knows if I am not a pastime to her more than she to me?

**—Montaigne**

❍❖❍

Some people say that cats are sneaky, evil, and cruel. True, and they have many other fine qualities as well.

**—Missy Dizick**

❍❖❍

The problem with cats is that they get the same exact look whether they see a moth or an axe-murderer.

**—Paula Poundstone**

❍❖❍

Cats are kindly masters, just so long as you remember your place.

**—Paul Gray**

❍❖❍

- One of the most striking differences between a cat and a lie is that a cat only has nine lives.
- Of all God's creatures, there is only one that cannot be made slave of the leash. That one is the cat. If man could be crossed with the cat it would improve the man, but it would deteriorate the cat.

**—Mark Twain**

❍❖❍

Women and cats will do as they please, and men and dogs should relax and get used to the idea.

**—Robert A Heinlein**

❍❖❍

The naming of cats is a difficult matter. It isn't just one of your holiday games. You may think at first I'm mad as a hatter, when I tell you a cat must have three different names...

**—TS Eliot**

❍❖❍

- Cats can be cooperative when something feels good which, to a cat, is the way everything is supposed to feel as much of the time as possible.
- Cats are a tonic, they are a laugh, they are a cuddle; they are at least pretty just about all of the time and beautiful some of the time.

**—Roger Caras**

❍❖❍

Curiosity killed the cat, but for a while I was a suspect.

**—Steven Wright**

❍❖❍

Cats always know whether people like or dislike them. They do not always care enough to do anything about it.

**—Winifred Carriere**

❍❖❍

Cats know how to obtain food without labour, shelter without confinement, and love without penalties.

**—WL George**

❍❖❍

A meow massages the heart.

**—Stuart McMillan**

❍❖❍

Cats are a mysterious kind of folk. There is more passing in their minds than we are aware of.

**—Sir Walter Scott**

❍❖❍

I am indebted to the cat for a particular kind of honourable deceit, for a greater control over myself, for a characteristic aversion to brutal sounds, and for the need to keep silent for long periods of time.

**—Colette**

❍❖❍

- A cat sees us as the dogs... A cat sees himself as the human.
- Thousands of years ago, cats were worshipped as gods. Cats have never forgotten this.
- Cat memory is a funny thing. We have a rollover cat. It's the one we send whenever anybody needs a cat to roll over. It's a smart cat and knows other tricks. But whenever it gets stressed out on the set it just keeps rolling over.
- There are many intelligent species in the universe. They are all owned by cats.
- If you yell at a cat, you're the one who is making a fool of yourself.
- There is no snooze button on a cat who wants breakfast.
- Cat's Motto: No matter what you've done wrong, always try to make it look like the dog did it.
- If God created man in His own image, you've got to wonder: in whose image did He create the nobler cat?

**—Anonymous**

# Divine Nature

What is man without the beasts? If all the beasts were gone, men would die from loneliness of spirit. For whatever happens to the beasts happens to man. All things are connected...

**—Chief Seattle**

❍❖❍

Nature is unfair? So much the better – inequality is the only bearable thing, the monotony of equality can only lead us to boredom.

**—Francis Pica**

❍❖❍

I believe in God, only I spell it Nature.

**—Frank Lloyd Wright**

❍❖❍

Nature is man's teacher. She unfolds her treasures to his search, unseals his eye, illumes his mind, and purifies his heart; an influence breathes from all the sights and sounds of her existence.

**—Alfred Billings Street**

❍❖❍

Respect the old and cherish the young. Even insects, grass and trees you must not hurt.

**—Ko Hung**

❍❖❍

Nature is slow, but sure; she works no faster than need be; she is the tortoise that wins the race by her perseverance.

**—Henry David Thoreau**

❍❖❍

At first a small line of inconceivable splendour emerged on the horizon which, quickly expanding, the sun appeared in all of his glory, unveiling the whole face of nature, vivifying every colour of the landscape, and sprinkling the dewy earth with glittering light.

**—Ann Radcliff**

❍❖❍

Nature as a poet, an enthusiastic working man, becomes more and more visible the farther and higher we go.

**—John Muir**

❍❖❍

Occurrences in this domain are beyond the reach of exact prediction because of the variety of factors in operation, not because of any lack of order in nature.

**—Albert Einstein**

❍❖❍

The best remedy for those who are afraid, lonely or unhappy is to go outside, somewhere where they can be quiet, alone with the heavens, nature and God. Because only then does one feel that all is as it should be and that God wishes to see people happy, amidst the simple beauty of nature.

**—Anne Frank**

❍❖❍

Anxiety and conscience are a powerful pair of dynamos. Between them, they have ensured that one shall work hard, but they cannot ensure that one shall work at anything worthwhile.

**—Arnold Toynbee**

❍❖❍

To see the earth as we now see it, small and beautiful in that eternal silence where it floats, is to see ourselves as riders on the earth together; brothers on that bright loveliness in the unending night – brothers who see now they are truly brothers.

**—Archibald MacLeish**

❍❖❍

I think it pisses God off if you walk by the colour purple in a field somewhere and don't take notice.

**—Alice Walker**

❍❖❍

We abuse land because we regard it as a commodity belonging to us. When we see land as a community to which we belong, we may begin to use it with love and respect.

**—Aldo Leopold**

❍❖❍

If a June night could talk, it would probably boast it invented romance.

**—Bern Williams**

❍❖❍

People who will not sustain trees will soon live in a world that will not sustain.

**—Bryce Nelson**

❍❖❍

To be overcome by the fragrance of flowers is a delectable form of defeat.

**—Beverly Nichols**

❍❖❍

We cannot think too highly of our nature, or too humbly of ourselves.

**—Colton**

❍❖❍

And how should a beautiful, ignorant stream of water know it heads for an early release – out across the desert, running toward the Gulf, below sea level, to murmur its lullaby, and see the Imperial Valley rise out of burning sand with cotton blossoms, wheat, watermelons, roses – how should it know?

**—Carl Sandburg**

❍❖❍

Nature always tends to act in the simplest way.

**—Bernoulli**

❍❖❍

For me, a landscape does not exist in its own right, since its appearance changes at every moment; but the surrounding atmosphere brings it to life – the light and the air, which vary continually. For me, it is only the surrounding atmosphere which gives subjects their true value.

**—Claude Monet**

I've made an odd discovery. Every time I talk to a savant, I feel quite sure that happiness is no longer a possibility. Yet when I talk with my gardener, I'm convinced of the opposite.

**—Bertrand Russell**

❍❖❍

*Talk not of temples, there is one*
*Built without hands, to mankind given;*
*Its lamps are the meridian sun*
*And all the stars of heaven,*
*Its walls are the cerulean sky,*
*Its floor the earth so green and fair,*
*The dome its immensity*
*All nature worships there.*

**—David Vedder**

❍❖❍

Nature gives to every time and season some beauties of its own; and from morning to night, as from the cradle to the grave, it is but a succession of changes so gentle and easy that we can scarcely mark their progress.

**—Charles Dickens**

❍❖❍

You can live for years next door to a big pine tree, honoured to have so venerable a neighbour, even when it sheds needles all over your flowers or wakes you, dropping big cones onto your deck at still of night.

**—Denise Levertov**

❍❖❍

I thank you God for this most amazing day, for the leaping greenly spirits of trees, and for the blue dream of sky and for everything which is natural, which is infinite, which is new.

**—Cummings**

❍❖❍

Go out, go out I beg of you. And taste the beauty of the wild. Behold the miracle of the earth. With all the wonder of a child.

**—Edna Jacques**

❍❖❍

All Nature speaks the voice of dissolution. The highway of history and of life is strewn with the wrecks that Time, the great despoiler, has made. We listen sorrowfully to the autumn winds as they sigh through dismantled forests, but we know their breath will be soft and vernal in the spring, and the dead flowers and withered foliage will blossom and bloom again. And if a man dies, shall he too, not live again?

**—Daniel Wolsey**

❍❖❍

The laws of nature are but the mathematical thoughts of God.

**—Euclid**

❍❖❍

Nothing living should ever be treated with contempt. Whatever it is that lives, a man, a tree, or a bird, should be touched gently, because time is short. Civilisation is another word for respect for life.

**—Elizabeth Goudge**

❍❖❍

Nature, like us, is sometimes caught without her diadem.

**—Emily Dickinson**

❍❖❍

Were I called on to define, very briefly, the term Art, I should call it 'the reproduction of what the Senses perceive in Nature through the veil of the soul'.

**—Edgar Allan Poe**

❍❖❍

- For man, autumn is a time of harvest, of gathering together. For nature, it is a time of sowing, of scattering abroad.
- Even the lifelong traveller knows but an infinitesimal portion of the Earth's surface. Those who have written best about the land and its wild inhabitants... have often been stay-at-home naturalists... concentrating their attention and affection on a relatively small area.

**—Edwin Way Teale**

❍❖❍

Lovers are fools, but nature makes them so.

**—Elbert Hubbard**

❍❖❍

Nature, to be commanded, must be obeyed.

**—Francis Bacon**

❍❖❍

Nature goes on her way, and all that to us seems an exception is really according to order.

**—Goethe**

❍❖❍

It is good to realise that if love and peace can prevail on earth, and if we can teach our children to honour nature's gifts, the joys and beauties of the outdoors will be here forever.

**—Jimmy Carter**

❍❖❍

I love to think of nature as an unlimited broadcasting station through which God speaks to us every hour, if we will only tune in.

**—George Washington Carver**

❍❖❍

*There is a pleasure in the pathless woods,*
*There is rapture on the lonely shore,*
*There is society, where none intrudes.*
*By the deep sea, and music in its roars;*
*I love not man the less, but nature more.*

**—Gordon**

❍❖❍

The earth's distances invite the eye. And as the eye reaches, so must the mind stretch to meet these new horizons. I challenge anyone to stand with autumn on a hilltop and fail to see a new expanse not only around him, but in him, too.

**—Hal Borland**

❍❖❍

If a man walks in the woods for love of them half of each day, he is in danger of being regarded as a loafer. But if he spends his days as a speculator, shearing off those woods and making the earth bald before her time, he is deemed an industrious and enterprising citizen.

**—Henry David Thoreau**

❍❖❍

To me a lush carpet of pine needles or spongy grass is more welcome than the most luxurious Persian rug.

**—Helen Keller**

❍❖❍

Who can explain the secret pathos of Nature's loveliness? It is a touch of melancholy inherited from our mother Eve. It is an unconscious memory of the lost Paradise. It is the sense that even if we should find another Eden, we would not be fit to enjoy it perfectly nor stay in it forever.

**—Henry van Dyke**

❍❖❍

- Every heart has its secret sorrows, which the world knows not, and oftentimes we call a man cold when he is only sad.
- The Laws of Nature are just, but terrible. There is no weak mercy in them. Cause and consequence are inseparable and inevitable. The elements have no forbearance. The fire burns, the water drowns, the air consumes, the earth buries. And perhaps it would be well for our race if the punishment of crimes against the Laws of Man were as inevitable as the punishment of crimes against the Laws of Nature – were Man as unerring in his judgments as Nature.
- *And nature, the old nurse, took*
  *The child upon her knee,*
  *Saying, 'Here is a story-book*
  *The Father has written for thee.'*
  *'Come, wander, with me,' she said,*
  *'Into regions yet untrod;*
  *And read what is still unread*
  *In the manuscripts of god.'*

**—Henry Wadsworth Longfellow**

❍❖❍

*I sit beside the fire and think of all that I have seen,*
*Of meadow flowers and butterflies in summers*
*that have been;*
*Of yellow leaves and gossamer in autumns that there were,*
*with morning mist and silver sun and wind upon my hair.*

**—JRR Tolkien**

What have we achieved in mowing down mountain ranges, harnessing the energy of mighty rivers, or moving whole populations about like chess pieces, if we ourselves remain the same restless, miserable, frustrated creatures we were before? To call such activity progress is utter delusion. We may succeed in altering the face of the earth until it is unrecognisable even to the Creator, but if we are unaffected wherein lies the meaning?

**—Henry Miller**

❍❖❍

Adapt or perish, now as ever, is nature's inexorable imperative.

**—HG Wells**

❍❖❍

Nature goes her own way and all that to us seems an exception is really according to order.

**—Johann Wolfgang von Goethe**

- Climb the mountains and get their good tidings. Nature's peace will flow into you as sunshine flows into trees. The winds will blow their own freshness into you, and the storms their energy, while cares will drop away from you like the leaves of autumn.
- The hills and groves were God's first temples, and the more they are cut down and hewn into cathedrals and churches, the farther off and dimmer seems the Lord himself.
- Nature is always lovely, invincible, glad, whatever is done and suffered by her creatures. All scars she heals, whether in rocks or water or sky or hearts.
- Thousands of tired, nerve-shaken, over-civilised people are beginning to find out that going to the mountains is going home; that wilderness is a necessity; and that mountain parks and reservations are useful not only as fountains of timber and irrigating rivers, but as fountains of life!

**—John Muir**

❍❖❍

Nature does not hurry, yet everything is accomplished.

**—Lao Tzu**

Nature is a collective idea and, though its essence exists in each individual of the species, can never in its perfection inhabit a single object.

**—Henry Fuseli**

❍❖❍

I must confess to a feeling of profound humility in the presence of a universe which transcends us at almost every point. I feel like a child who, while playing by the seashore, has found a few bright coloured shells and a few pebbles while the whole vast ocean of truth stretches out almost untouched and unruffled before my eager fingers.

**—Isaac Newton**

❍❖❍

The human mind is not capable of grasping the Universe. We are like a little child entering a huge library. The walls are covered to the ceilings with books in many different tongues. The child knows that someone must have written these books. It does not know who or how. It does not understand the languages in which they are written. But the child notes a definite plan in the arrangement of books – a mysterious order that it does not comprehend, but only dimly suspects.

**—Albert Einstein**

❍❖❍

I willingly confess to so great a partiality for trees as tempts me to respect a man in exact proportion to his respect for them.

**—James Russell Lowell**

❍❖❍

One secret of success in observing nature's capacity to take a hint; a hair may show where a lion is hid. One must put this and that together, and value bits and shreds. Much alloy exists with the truth. The gold of nature does not look like gold at the first glance. It must be smelted and refined in the mind of the observer. And one must crush mountains of quartz and wash hills of sand to get to it.

**—John Burroughs**

❍❖❍

Nature never deceives us; it is always we who deceive ourselves.

**—Rousseau**

For in the true nature of things, if we rightly consider, every green tree is far more glorious than if it were made of gold and silver.

**—Martin Luther**

❍❖❍

Nature often holds up a mirror so we can see more clearly the ongoing processes of growth, renewal, and transformation in our lives.

**—Mary Ann Brussat**

❍❖❍

Nature has no mercy at all. Nature says, 'I'm going to snow. If you have on a bikini and no snowshoes, that's tough. I am going to snow anyway.'

**—Maya Angelou**

❍❖❍

Everything in the world has a hidden meaning—
Men, animals, trees, stars, they are all hieroglyphics.
When you see them you do not understand them.
You think they are really men, animals, trees, stars.
It is only years later that you understand.

**—Nikos Kazantzakis**

❍❖❍

Nature, whose sweet rains fall on just and unjust alike, will have clefts in the rocks where I may hide, and secret valleys in whose silence I may weep undetected. She will hang the night with stars so that I may walk abroad in the darkness without stumbling, and send the wind over my footprints so that none may track me to my hurt: she will cleanse me in great waters, and with bitter herbs make me whole.

**—Oscar Wilde**

❍❖❍

It is not so much for its beauty that the forest makes a claim upon men's hearts, as for that subtle something, that quality of air, that emanation from old trees, that so wonderfully charges and renews a weary spirit.

**—Robert Louis Stevenson**

❍❖❍

The day, water, sun, moon, night... I do not have to purchase these things with money.

**—Plautus**

❍❖❍

How cunningly nature hides every wrinkle of her inconceivable antiquity under roses and violets and morning dew!

**—Ralph Waldo Emerson**

❍❖❍

*We shall not cease from exploration*
*And the end of all our exploring,*
*Will be to arrive where we started*
*And know the place for the first time.*

**—TS Eliot**

❍❖❍

*So careful of the type she seems,*
*So careless of the single life.*

**—Lord Alfred Tennyson**

❍❖❍

To waste, to destroy, our natural resources, to skin and exhaust the land instead of using it so as to increase its usefulness, will result in undermining in the days of our children the very prosperity which we ought by right to hand down to them amplified and developed.

**—Theodore Roosevelt**

❍❖❍

The universe is composed of subjects to be communed with, not objects to be exploited. Everything has its own voice. Thunder and lightning and stars and planets, flowers, birds, animals, trees – all these have voices, and they constitute a community of existence that is profoundly related.

**—Thomas Berry**

❍❖❍

Sit down before fact like a little child, and be prepared to give up every preconceived notion. Follow humbly wherever and to whatever abyss Nature leads, or you shall learn nothing.

**—Thomas H Huxley**

❍❖❍

If one really loves nature, one can find beauty everywhere.

**—Vincent van Gogh**

❍❖❍

- Great things are done when men and mountains meet.
- *To see the world in a grain of sand*
  *And heaven in a wild flower,*
  *Hold infinity in the palm of your hand*
  *And eternity in an hour.*
- The tree which moves some to tears of joy is, in the eyes of others, only a green thing that stands in the way. Some see Nature all ridicule and deformity, and by these I shall not regulate my proportions; and some scarce see Nature at all. But to the eyes of the Man of Imagination, Nature is Imagination itself.

**—William Blake**

❍❖❍

April hath put a spirit of youth in everything.

**—William Shakespeare**

❍❖❍

- I am at two with nature.
- Of all the wonders of nature, a tree in summer is perhaps the most remarkable, with the possible exception of a moose singing 'Embraceable You' in spats.

**—Woody Allen**

❍❖❍

*Truth and love are my law and worship;*
*Form and conscience my manifestation and guide;*
*Nature and peace are my shelter and companion;*
*Order is my attitude;*
*Beauty and perfection are my attack.*

**—Wayne Krame**

❍❖❍

*Nature never betray'd,*
*The heart that loved her.*

**—William Wordsworth**

❍❖❍

Sundown is the hour for many strange effects in light and shade – enough to make a colourist go delirious – long spokes of molten silver sent horizontally through the trees, each leaf and branch of endless foliage a lit-up miracle, then lying all prone on the youthful, ripe, interminable grass, and giving the blades not only aggregate but individual splendour, in ways unknown to any other hour.

**—Walt Whitman**

❍❖❍

- The miracles of nature do not seem miracles because they are so common. If no one had ever seen a flower, even a dandelion would be the most startling event in the world.
- Though we travel the world over to find the beautiful, we must carry it with us or we find it not.
- *There's a whisper on the night-wind,*
  *There's a star agleam to guide us*
  *And the Wild is calling, calling...*

**—Anonymous**

# The Magic of Flowers

Autumn is a second spring when every leaf is a flower.

**—Albert Camus**

❍❖❍

I perhaps owe having become a painter to flowers.

**—Claude Monet**

❍❖❍

Flowers are without hope. Because hope is tomorrow and flowers have no tomorrow.

**—Antonio Porchia**

❍❖❍

If dandelions were hard to grow, they would be most welcome on any lawn.

**—Andrew Mason**

❍❖❍

All my life I have tried to pluck a thistle and plant a flower wherever the flower would grow, in thought and mind.

**—Abraham Lincoln**

❍❖❍

*Keep not your roses for my dead, cold brow*
*The way is lonely,*
*Let me feel them now.*

**—Arabella Smith**

❍❖❍

Every flower is a soul blossoming in Nature.

**—Gerard de Nerval**

❍❖❍

In the hope of reaching the moon, men fail to see the flowers that blossom at their feet.

**—Albert Schweitzer**

❍❖❍

How many flowers there are which only serve to produce essences, which could have been made into savoury dishes.

**—Charles Pierre Monselet**

❍❖❍

- Flowers are the sweetest things that God ever made, and forgot to put a soul into.
- Flowers have an expression of countenance as much as men or animals. Some seem to smile; some have a sad expression; some are pensive and diffident; others again are plain, honest and upright, like the broad-faced sunflower and the hollyhock.

**—Henry Ward Beecher**

❍❖❍

The temple bell stops but I still hear the sound coming out of the flowers.

**—Basho**

❍❖❍

*The kiss of the sun for pardon,*
*The song of the birds for mirth.*
*One is nearer God's heart in a garden,*
*Than anywhere else on earth.*

**—Dorothy Gurney**

❍❖❍

Every rose has its thorn: You never find a woman without pins and needles.

**—Douglas Jerrolds**

❍❖❍

The best rosebush, after all, is not that which has the fewest thorns, but that which bears the finest roses.

**—Henry van Dyke**

❍❖❍

No path of flowers leads to glory.

**—Jean de La Fontaine**

❍❖❍

Flowers never emit so sweet and strong a fragrance as before a storm. When a storm approaches thee, be as fragrant as a sweet-smelling flower.

**—Jean Paul Richter**

❍❖❍

The flower is the poetry of reproduction. It is an example of the eternal seductiveness of life.

**—Jean Giraudoux**

❍❖❍

- Flowers seem intended for a solace of ordinary humanity.
- The actual flower is the plant's highest fulfilment, and is not here exclusively for herbaria, county floras and plant geography: flowers are here first of all for delight.

**—John Ruskin**

❍❖❍

We must learn not to disassociate the airy flower from the earthy root, for the flower that is cut off from its root fades, and its seeds are barren, whereas the root, secure in mother earth, can produce flower after flower and bring their fruit to maturity.

**—Kabbalah**

❍❖❍

The silence of a flower: a kind of silence, which we continually evade, of which we find only the shadow in dreams.

**—Lewis Thompson**

❍❖❍

*And with childlike credulous affection,*
*We behold their tender buds expand.*
*Emblems of our own great resurrection,*
*Emblems of the bright and better land.*

**—Henry Wadsworth Longfellow**

❍❖❍

Flowers have spoken to me more than I can tell in written words. They are the hieroglyphics of angels, loved by all men for the beauty of their character, though few can decipher even fragments of their meaning.

**—Lydia M Child**

❍❖❍

*Flower in the crannied wall,*
*I pluck you out of the crannies—*
*Hold you here, root and all, in my hand,*
*Little flower – but if I could understand*
*What you are, root and all, and all in all,*
*I should know what God and man is.*

**—Lord Alfred Tennyson**

❍❖❍

- Earth laughs in flowers.
- Flowers... are a proud assertion that a ray of beauty out-values all the utilities of the world.
- There is simply the rose; it is perfect in every moment of its existence.

**—Ralph Waldo Emerson**

❍❖❍

Flowers always make people better, happier and more helpful; they are sunshine, food and medicine to the soul.

**—Luther Burbank**

❍❖❍

Whatever a man's age, he can reduce it several years by putting a bright-coloured flower in his buttonhole.

**—Mark Twain**

❍❖❍

An old friend is like a full-blown rose, each velvet petal a pleasant memory. Its fragrance recalls sweetness that grows with years of love, understanding and sympathy.

**—Margaret Trenton Crawford**

❍❖❍

The Amen of Nature is always a flower.

**—Oliver Wendell Holmes**

❍❖❍

*Gather ye rosebuds while ye may*
*Old time is still a-flying*
*And this same flower that smiles today*
*Tomorrow will be dying.*

**—Robert Herrick**

❍❖❍

By plucking her petals, you do not gather the beauty of the flower.

**—Rabindranath Tagore**

❍❖❍

*I have a garden of my own,*
*Shining with flowers of every hue;*
*I loved it dearly while alone,*
*But I shall love it more with you;*
*And there the golden bees shall come,*
*In summer time at the break of morn,*
*And wake us with their busy hum*
*Around the Siha's fragrant thorn.*

**—Thomas Moore**

❍❖❍

*The flower invites the butterfly with no-mind,*
*The butterfly visits the flower with no-mind.*
*The flower opens, the butterfly comes;*
*The butterfly comes, the flower opens.*
*I don't know others,*
*Others don't know me.*
*By not knowing we follow nature's course.*

**—Ryokan**

❍❖❍

*Flowers are lovely;*
*Love is flower-like*
*Friendship is a sheltering tree.*

**—Samuel Taylor Coleridge**

❍❖❍

The honey from the flowers of the senses,
Ever present within, the ruler of time,
Goes beyond fear.
For this Self is Supreme!

**—Upanishad**

❍❖❍

Life is the flower for which love is the honey.

**—Victor Hugo**

❍❖❍

- To me the meanest flower that blows can give
  Thoughts that do often lie too deep for tears.
- *How does the meadow flower its bloom unfold?*
  *Because the lovely little flower is free*
  *Down to its root*
  *And in that freedom, hold.*
- This is my faith that every flower
  Enjoys the air it breathes!

**—William Wordsworth**

❍❖❍

*Pluck not the wayside flower;*
*It is the traveller's dower.*

**—William Allingham**

❍❖❍

Flowers are beautiful hieroglyphics of nature, with which she indicates how much she loves us.

**—Wolfgang von Goethe**

❍❖❍

- A thousand flowers
  Each seeming one
  That learnt by gazing at the sun.
- Creativity is so delicate a flower
  that praise tends to make it bloom...

**—Anonymous**

# Cow Tales

The cow knows not what her tail is worth till she has lost it.

**—George Herbert**

❍❖❍

You can only milk a cow so long, and then you're left holding the pail.

**—Hank Aaron**

❍❖❍

Keep a cow, and the milk won't have to be watered but once.

**—Josh Billings**

❍❖❍

Why keep a cow when there's milk available in the market?

**—Bachelor's Saying**

❍❖❍

Sacred cows make the best hamburgers.

**—Mark Twain**

❍❖❍

My cow milks me.

**—Ralph Waldo Emerson**

❍❖❍

A cow is a very good animal in the field; but we turn her out of a garden.

**—Samuel Johnson**

❍❖❍

Cows are amongst the gentlest of breathing creatures; none shows more passionate tenderness to their young when deprived of them; and I am not ashamed to profess a deep love for these quiet creatures.

**—Thomas de Quince**

# Elephant Talk

Elephant: A mouse built to government specifications.

**—Lazarus Long**

❍❖❍

A king who always cares for the elephants like his own sons is always victorious and will enjoy the friendship of the celestial world after death.

**—Kautilya**

❍❖❍

When an elephant is in trouble even a frog will kick him.

**—Hindi Proverb**

❍❖❍

When elephants fight, it is the grass that suffers.

**—African Proverb**

❍❖❍

The dog is man's companion; the elephant is his slave.

**—Sir Samuel Baker**

❍❖❍

What is bigger than an elephant? But this also has become man's plaything, and a spectacle at public solemnities; and it learns to skip, dance, and kneel.

**—Plutarch**

❍❖❍

Watch a human being walk through a bush, and it is a messy business. Watch an elephant encounter a thicket of twigs and thorns, and he seems to flow through it.

**—Anthony Smith**

# Horse Sense

Why, I'd horsewhip you if I had a horse.

**—Groucho Marx**

❍❖❍

For the want of a nail, the shoe was lost; for the want of a shoe, the horse was lost; and for the want of a horse, the rider was lost, being overtaken and slain by the enemy, all for the want of care about a horseshoe nail.

**—Benjamin Franklin**

❍❖❍

Many people have sighed for the 'good old days' and regretted the 'passing of the horse', but today, when only those who like horses own them, it is a far better time for horses.

**—CW Anderson**

❍❖❍

Far back, far back in our dark soul the horse prances... The horse, the horse! The symbol of surging potency and power of movement, of action.

**—DH Lawrence**

❍❖❍

Treat a horse like a woman and a woman like a horse. And they'll both win for you.

**—Elizabeth Arden**

❍❖❍

Old minds are like old horses; you must exercise them if you wish to keep them in working order.

**—John Adams**

❍❖❍

Horses and jockeys mature earlier than people – which is why horses are admitted to race tracks at the age of two, and jockeys before they are old enough to shave.

**—Dick Deddoes**

❍❖❍

Never ride your horse more than five-and-thirty miles a day, always taking more care of him than of yourself; which is right and reasonable, seeing as how the horse is the best animal of the two.

**—George Borrow**

❍❖❍

I can always tell which is the front end of a horse, but beyond that, my art is not above the ordinary.

**—Mark Twain**

❍❖❍

A horse doesn't care how much you know until he knows how much you care.

**—Pat Parelli**

❍❖❍

No ride is ever the last one. No horse is ever the last one you will have. Somehow there will always be other horses, other places to ride them.

**—Monica Dickens**

❍❖❍

- A mule is just like a horse, but even more so.
- A horse! A horse! My kingdom for a horse!

**—William Shakespeare**

❍❖❍

When God created the horse, he said to the magnificent creature: I have made thee as no other. All the treasures of the earth shall lie between thy eyes. Thou shalt cast thy enemies between thy hooves, but thou shalt carry my friends upon thy back. Thy saddle shall be the seat of prayers to me. And thou will fly without any wings, and conquer without any sword.

**—The Koran**

Horses change lives. They give our young people confidence and self-esteem. They provide peace and tranquillity to troubled souls – they give us hope!

**—Toni Robinson**

❍❖❍

A horse gallops with his lungs,
Perseveres with his heart,
And wins with his character.

**—Tesio**

❍❖❍

There is something about the outside of a horse that is good for the inside of a man.

**—Winston Churchill**

❍❖❍

Horse sense is the thing a horse has which keeps it from betting on people.

**—WC Fields**

❍❖❍

- A horse is such a thing of beauty... None will tire of looking at him as long as he displays himself in his splendour.
- If one induces the horse to assume that carriage which it would adopt of its own accord when displaying its beauty, then, one directs the horse to appear joyous and magnificent, proud and remarkable for having been ridden.

**—Xenophon**

❍❖❍

- If you want a kitten, start out asking for a horse.
- For a horse with a solid head, don't try to break it through with a mallet, try to melt it with sugar!
- You can lead a horse to water but you can't make him backstroke.
- *A man of kindness to his horse, is kind*
  *But brutal actions show a brutal mind.*
  *He was designed thy servant, not thy drudge.*
  *Remember his creator is thy judge.*

**—Anonymous**

## Mouse Moves

When rats leave a sinking ship, where exactly do they think they're going?

**—Douglas Gauck**

❍❖❍

*A mouse that prayed for Allah's aid*
*Blasphemed when no such aid befell;*
*A cat who feasted on that mouse*
*Thought Allah managed vastly well.*

**—Saki**

❍❖❍

Anyone who has invented a better mousetrap, or the contemporary equivalent, can expect to be harassed by strangers demanding that you read their unpublished manuscripts or undergo the humiliation of public speaking, usually on remote Midwestern campuses.

**—Barbara Ehrenreich**

❍❖❍

Women do not like timid men. Cats do not like prudent rats.

**—John Webb**

❍❖❍

Alcohol removes inhibitions – like that scared little mouse who got drunk, shook his whiskers and shouted: "Now bring on that damn cat!"

**—Eleanor Early**

❍❖❍

Rats greet you, they interact, they try to please. They are as close to a dog as you're going to get in a rodent.

**—Elizabeth Fucci**

# Porky Pig

The pig is bigger
Than we had thought
And not so pink,
Fringed with white
Hairs that look
Grey, because while
They say a pig is clean,
It is not always; still,
We like this cheerful,
Rich, soft-bellied beast –
It wants to be comfortable.

**—Valerie Worth**

❍❖❍

Pigs are very beautiful animals... There is no point of view from which a really corpulent pig is not full of sumptuous and satisfying curves.

**—GK Chesterton**

❍❖❍

You can put wings on a pig, but you don't make it an eagle.

**—Bill Clinton**

❍❖❍

- Feed a pig and you'll have a hog.
- A pretty pig makes an ugly old sow.
- Give to a pig when it grunts and a child when it cries, and you will have a fine pig and a bad child.

**—Proverbs**

# The Question of Beauty

- Beauty is all very well at first sight; but who ever looks at it when it has been in the house three days?
- I hope you have lost your good looks, for while they last any fool can adore you, and the adoration of fools is bad for the soul. No, give me a ruined complexion and a lost figure and sixteen chins on a farmyard of crow's feet and an obvious wig. Then you shall see me coming out strong.

**—George Bernard Shaw**

❍❖❍

Let us worry about beauty first, and truth will take care of itself.

**—A Zee**

❍❖❍

In nature, nothing is perfect and everything is perfect. Trees can be contorted, bent in weird ways, and they're still beautiful.

**—Alice Walker**

❍❖❍

- Beauty is the gift of God.
- Personal beauty is a greater recommendation than any letter of reference.
- Beauty depends on size as well as symmetry. No very small animal can be beautiful, for looking at it takes so small a portion of time that the impression of it will be confused. Nor can any very large one, for a whole view of it cannot be had at once.

**—Aristotle**

❍❖❍

Even beauties can be unattractive. If you catch a beauty in the wrong light at the right time, forget it. I believe in low lights and trick mirrors. I believe in plastic surgery.

**—Andy Warhol**

❍❖❍

The most beautiful thing we can experience is the mysterious. It is the source of all true art and all science. He to whom this emotion is a stranger, who can no longer pause to wonder and stand rapt in awe, is as good as dead: his eyes are closed.

**—Albert Einstein**

❍❖❍

Beauty is an experience, nothing else. It is not a fixed pattern or an arrangement of features. It is something felt, a glow or a communicated sense of fineness. What ails us is that our sense of beauty is so bruised and blunted, we miss all the best.

**—DH Lawrence**

❍❖❍

People are like stained glass windows: they sparkle and shine when the sun is out, but when the darkness sets in their true beauty is revealed only if there is a light within.

**—Elizabeth Kubler-Ross**

❍❖❍

Nature gives to every time and season some beauties of its own.

**—Charles Dickens**

❍❖❍

Everything has beauty, but not everyone sees it.

**—Confucius**

❍❖❍

To be surrounded by beautiful things has much influence upon the human creature; to make beautiful things has more.

**—Charlotte Perkins Gilman**

❍❖❍

Zest is the secret of all beauty. There is no beauty that is attractive without zest.

**—Christian Dior**

❍❖❍

If you're considered a beauty, it's hard to be accepted doing anything but standing around.

**—Cybil Shepard**

Never lose an opportunity of seeing anything that is beautiful, for beauty is God's handwriting, a wayside sacrament.

**—Emerson**

Most of us have had moments in childhood when we touched the divine presence. We did not think it extraordinary because it wasn't; it was just a beautiful moment filled with love. In those simple moments our hearts were alive, and we saw the poignant beauty of life vividly with wonder and appreciation.

**—David and Bruce McArthur**

Beauty is power; a smile is its sword.

**—Charles Reade**

Walk on a rainbow trail; walk on a trail of song, and all about you will be beauty. There is a way out of every dark mist, over a rainbow trail.

**—Edward A Navajo**

- There is no excellent beauty that hath not some strangeness in the proportion.
- Beauty is as summer fruits, which are easy to corrupt and cannot last; and for the most part it makes a dissolute youth, and an age a little out of countenance; but if it lights well, it makes virtue shine and vice blush.

**—Francis Bacon**

Beauty itself is but the sensible image of the Infinite. Like truth and justice it lives within us; like virtue and the moral law it is a companion of the soul.

**—George Bancroft**

❍❖❍

There are various orders of beauty, causing men to make fools of themselves in various styles... but there is one order of beauty which seems made to turn the heads not only of men, but of all intelligent mammals, even of women.

It is a beauty like that of kittens, or very small downy ducks making gentle rippling noises with their soft bills, or babies just beginning to toddle and to engage in conscious mischief – a beauty with which you can never be angry, but that you feel ready to crush for inability to comprehend the state of mind into which it throws you.

**—George Eliot**

❍❖❍

The best and most beautiful things in the world cannot be seen or even touched. They must be felt with the heart.

**—Helen Keller**

❍❖❍

Beauty and sadness always go together.
Nature thought beauty too rich to go forth
upon the earth without a meet alloy.

**—George MacDonald**

❍❖❍

The beauty that addresses itself to the eyes is only the spell of the moment; the eye of the body is not always that of the soul.

**—George Sand**

❍❖❍

Beauty is whatever gives joy.

**—Hugh Nibley**

❍❖❍

The first question I ask myself when something doesn't seem to be beautiful is why do I think it's not beautiful. And very shortly you discover that there is no reason.

**—John Cage**

❍❖❍

Nothing is beautiful from every point of view.

**—Horace**

❍❖❍

It is something to be able to paint a particular picture, or to carve a statue, and so to make a few objects beautiful; but it is far more glorious to carve and paint the very atmosphere and medium through which we look, which morally we can do. To affect the quality of the day, that is the highest of arts.

**—Henry David Thoreau**

❍❖❍

Beauty is the promise of happiness.

**—B Henri Stendhal**

❍❖❍

- Beauty is truth, truth beauty; that is all ye know on earth, and all ye need to know.
- *A thing of beauty is a joy forever:*  
  *Its loveliness increases;*  
  *It will never pass into nothingness.*

**—John Keats**

❍❖❍

My heart that was rapt away by the wild cherry blossoms – will it return to my body when they scatter?

**—Kotomichi**

❍❖❍

- Beauty is not in the face; beauty is a light in the heart.
- Beauty is eternity gazing at itself in a mirror.
- *All these things have you said of beauty.*  
  *Yet in truth you spoke not of her but of needs unsatisfied,*  
  *And beauty is not a need but an ecstasy.*  
  *It is not a mouth thirsting nor an empty hand stretched forth,*  
  *But rather a heart inflamed and a soul enchanted.*  
  *It is not the image you would see nor the song you would hear,*  
  *But rather an image you see though you close your eyes*  
  *And a song you hear though you shut your ears.*

**—Kahlil Gibran**

I still find each day too short for all the thoughts I want to think, all the walks I want to take, all the books I want to read, and all the friends I want to see. The longer I live the more my mind dwells upon the beauty and wonder of the world. I hardly know which feeling leads – wonderment or admiration.

**—John Burroughs**

❍❖❍

*There's beauty in the way she looks*
*There's beauty in her heart*
*There's beauty in the way she thinks*
*That sets our Jane apart.*

**—Keith Logan**

❍❖❍

What a strange illusion it is to suppose that beauty is goodness.

**—Leo Tolstoy**

Whatever is in any way beautiful hath its source of beauty in itself, and is complete in itself; praise forms no part of it. So it is none the worse nor the better for being praised.

**—Marcus Aurelius**

- Tell them dear, that if eyes were made for seeing, then beauty is its own excuse for being.
- We ascribe beauty to that which is simple; which has no superfluous parts; which exactly answers its end; which stands related to all things; which is the means of many extremes.
- The criterion of true beauty is that it increases on examination; if false, that it lessens. There is, therefore, something in true beauty that corresponds with right reason, and is not the mere creation of fancy.
- Never lose an opportunity of seeing anything that is beautiful, for beauty is God's handwriting – a wayside sacrament. Welcome it in every fair face, in every fair sky, in every flower, and thank God for it as a cup of blessing.

**—Ralph Waldo Emerson**

Beauty is the soul shining from the eyes.

—**Merle Shain**

❍❖❍

Beauty is the purgation of superfluities.

—**Michelangelo**

❍❖❍

Keep your faith in all beautiful things;
in the sun when it is hidden, in the spring when it is gone.

—**Roy R Wilson**

❍❖❍

It is only a little planet, but how beautiful it is.

—**Robinson Jeffers**

❍❖❍

Beauty is a short-lived tyranny.

—**Socrates**

❍❖❍

- *What a piece of work is a man!*
  *How noble in reason, how infinite in faculty, in form and moving,*
  *How express and admirable in action,*
  *How like an angel, in apprehension*
  *How like a god – the beauty of the world, the paragon of animals!*
- *To me, fair friend, you never can be old,*
  *For as you were when first your eye I eyed,*
  *Such seems your beauty still.*
- *Shall I compare thee to a summer's day?*
  *Thou art more lovely and more temperate;*
  *Rough winds do shake the darling buds of May,*
  *And summer's lease hath all too.*

—**William Shakespeare**

❍❖❍

The beauty of the world has two edges, one of laughter, one of anguish, cutting the heart asunder.

—**Virginia Woolf**

❍❖❍

Harmony and beauty of the mind and soul, harmony and beauty of thoughts and feelings, harmony and beauty in every outward act and movement, harmony and beauty of life and surroundings, this is the demand of Mahalakshmi.

**—Sri Aurobindo**

❍❖❍

The definition of a beautiful woman is one who loves me.

**—Sloan Wilson**

❍❖❍

- Beauty is an ecstasy; it is as simple as hunger. There is really nothing to be said about it. It is like the perfume of a rose; you can smell it and that is all.
- The ideal has many names, and beauty is but one of them.

**—W Somerset Maugham**

❍❖❍

Every piece of the universe, even the tiniest little snow crystal, matters somehow. I have a place in the pattern, and so do you...

**—TG Barron**

❍❖❍

It is not sufficient to see and to know the beauty of a work. We must feel and be affected by it.

**—Voltaire**

❍❖❍

If you truly love Nature, you will find beauty everywhere.

**—Vincent van Gogh**

❍❖❍

Exuberance is beauty.

**—William Blake**

❍❖❍

*God scatters beauty as he scatters flowers*
*O'er the wide earth, and tells us all are ours.*
*A hundred lights in every temple burn,*
*And at each shrine I bend my knee in turn.*

**—Walter Savage Landor**

❍❖❍

- Beauty is not real. Beauty only exists in perception.
- The ugly may be beautiful, the pretty never.
- It's beauty that captures your attention, personality that captures your heart.
- Beauty lies in the specific looks of a person, rather than the object, because different people feel beauty in different things.

**—Anonymous**

# The Call of Birds

God loved the birds and invented trees. Man loved the birds and invented cages.

**—Jacques Deval**

❍❖❍

It is not only fine feathers that make fine birds.

**—Aesop**

❍❖❍

- *Sweet bird that shunn'st the noise of folly,*
  *Most musical, most melancholy!*
- *While the cock with lively din*
  *Scatters the rear of darkness thin,*
  *And to the stack, or the barn door,*
  *Stoutly struts his dames before.*

**—John Milton**

❍❖❍

To me, the garden is a doorway to other worlds; one of them, of course, is the world of birds. The garden is their dinner table, bursting with bugs and worms and succulent berries.

**—Anne Raver**

❍❖❍

Poor indeed is the garden in which birds find no homes.

**—Abram L Urban**

❍❖❍

Never look for birds of this year in the nests of the last.

**—Cervantes**

❍❖❍

A bird does not sing because it has an answer. It sings because it has a song.

**—Chinese Proverb**

❍❖❍

I hope you love birds too. It is economical. It saves going to heaven.

**—Emily Dickinson**

❍❖❍

Use the talents you possess – for the woods would be a very silent place if no birds sang except for the best.

**—Henry van Dyke**

❍❖❍

How come the dove gets to be the peace symbol? How about the pillow? It has more feathers than the dove, and it doesn't have that dangerous beak.

**—Jack Handey**

❍❖❍

- Hummingbirds have forgotten the words.
- A bird in the hand does it on your wrist.

**—Graffiti**

❍❖❍

A feather in the hand is better than a bird in the air.

**—George Herbert**

❍❖❍

A turkey is more occult and awful than all the angels and archangels. Insofar as God has partly revealed to us an angelic world, he has partly told us what an angel means. But God has never told us what a turkey means. And if you go and stare at a live turkey for an hour or two, you will find by the end of it that the enigma has rather increased than diminished.

**—Gilbert K Chesterton**

❍❖❍

I value my garden more for being full of blackbirds than of cherries, and very frankly give them fruit for their songs.

**—Joseph Addison**

❍❖❍

Shoot all the blue jays you want, if you can hit 'em, but remember it's a sin to kill a mockingbird.

**—Harper Lee**

❍❖❍

- The bluebird carries the sky on his back.
- I once had a sparrow alight upon my shoulder for a moment, while I was hoeing in a village garden, and I felt that I was more distinguished by that circumstance than I should have been by any epaulet I could have worn.

**—Henry David Thoreau**

❍❖❍

*Sweet bird! Thy bow'r is evergreen,*
*Thy sky is ever clear;*
*Thou hast no sorrow in thy song,*
*No winter in thy year.*

**—John Logan**

❍❖❍

When nature made the bluebird she wished to propitiate both the sky and the earth, so she gave him the colour of the one on his back and the hue of the other on his breast.

**—John Burroughs**

❍❖❍

Look at that mallard as he floats on the lake, see his elevated head glittering with emerald green, his amber eyes glancing in the light! Even at this distance, he has marked you, and suspects that you bear no goodwill towards him, for he sees that you have a gun, and he has many a time been frightened by its report, or that of some other. The wary bird draws his feet under his body, springs upon them, opens his wings, and with loud quacks bids you farewell.

**—John James Audubon**

*Hold fast to dreams,*
*For if dreams die*
*Life is a broken-winged bird,*
*That cannot fly.*

**—Langston Hughes**

Spring would not be spring without bird-songs.

**—Francis M Chapman**

❍❖❍

- A poet is a bird of unearthly excellence, who escapes from his celestial realm and arrives in this world warbling. If we do not cherish him, he spreads his wings and flies back into his homeland.
- The bird has an honour that man does not have. Man lives in the traps of his abdicated laws and traditions; but the birds live according to the natural law of God who causes the earth to turn around the sun.

**—Kahlil Gibran**

❍❖❍

Bats have no bankers and they do not drink and cannot be arrested and pay no tax and, in general, bats have it made.

**—John Berryman**

❍❖❍

*The caged bird sings*
*with a fearful trill*
*Of things unknown*
*but longed for still*
*And his tune is heard*
*on the distant hill*
*For the caged bird*
*sings of freedom.*

**—Maya Angelou**

❍❖❍

We never miss the music until the sweet voiced bird has flown.

**—O Henry**

❍❖❍

*There was an old owl, who lived in an oak*
*The more he heard, the less he spoke;*
*The less he spoke, the more he heard*
*O, if men were all like that wise bird!*

**—Punch**

❍❖❍

*The silver swan, who living had no note,*
*When death approached, unlocked her silent throat.*

**—Orlando Gibbons**

❍❖❍

Everyone wants to understand painting. Why is there no attempt to understand the song of the birds?

**—Pablo Picasso**

❍❖❍

There is nothing in which the birds differ more from man than the way in which they can build and yet leave a landscape as it was before.

**—Robert Lynd**

❍❖❍

Birds sing after a storm; why shouldn't people feel as free to delight in whatever remains to them?

**—Rose F Kennedy**

❍❖❍

A nightingale dies of shame if another bird sings better.

**—Robert Burton**

❍❖❍

At the sight of blackbirds
Flying in a green light,
Even the bawds of euphony
Would cry out sharply.

**—Wallace Stevens**

❍❖❍

**To the Cuckoo**

- *Thrice welcome, darling of the spring!*
  *Even yet thou art to me*
  *No bird, but an invisible thing,*
  *A voice, a mystery.*
- *O Cuckoo! Shall I call thee a bird,*
  *Or but a wandering voice?*

**—William Wordsworth**

❍❖❍

- No bird soars too high if he soars with his own wings.
- *A robin redbreast in a cage,*
  *Puts all heaven in a rage.*

**—William Blake**

❍❖❍

There is a bird who by his coat,
And by the hoarseness of his note,
Might be supposed a crow.

**—William Cowper**

❍❖❍

- A bird in hand can make an awful mess.
- The early bird gets the worm, but the second mouse gets the cheese.

**—Anonymous**

# Beautiful Butterflies

Butterflies… flowers that fly and all but sing.

**—Robert Frost**

❍❖❍

The butterfly counts not months but moments, and has time enough.

**—Rabindranath Tagore**

❍❖❍

We are like butterflies who flutter for a day and think it is forever.

**—Carl Sagan**

❍❖❍

I became the butterfly. I got out of the cocoon, and I flew.

**—Lynn Redgrave**

❍❖❍

Once upon a time, I dreamt I was a butterfly, fluttering hither and thither, to all intents and purposes a butterfly… suddenly I awoke… Now I do not know whether I was tnen a man dreaming I was a butterfly, or whether I am now a butterfly dreaming I am a man.

**—Chuang Tzu**

❍❖❍

A butterfly alights beside us like a sunbeam,
and for a brief moment its glory and beauty
belong to our world. But then it flies on again,
and though we wish it could have stayed,
we feel lucky to have seen it at all.

**—Anonymous**

## Season's Greetings

Spring being a tough act to follow, God created June.

**—Al Bernstein**

❍❖❍

The acrid scents of autumn,
Reminiscent of slinking beasts, make me fear.

**—DH Lawrence**

❍❖❍

Spring is when you feel like whistling even with a shoe full of slush.

**—Doug Larson**

❍❖❍

Autumn into winter, winter into spring,
Spring into summer, summer into fall—
So rolls the changing year, and so we change;
Motion so swift, we know not that we move.

**—Dinah Maria Mulock**

❍❖❍

Autumn arrives in early morning, but spring at the close of a winter day.

**—Elizabeth Bowen**

❍❖❍

In a way winter is the real spring, the time when the inner things happen, the resurge of nature.

**—Edna O'Brien**

❍❖❍

- *A little madness in the spring,*
  *Is wholesome even for the King.*
- *There's a certain slant of light,*
  *Winter afternoons—*
  *That oppresses, like the heft*
  *Of cathedral tunes.*

**—Emily Dickinson**

❍❖❍

Every mile is two in winter.

**—George Herbert**

❍❖❍

Delicious autumn! My very soul is wedded to it, and if I were a bird, I would fly about the earth seeking the successive autumns.

**—George Eliot**

❍❖❍

*Listen! The wind is rising,*
*And the air is wild with leaves,*
*We have had our summer evenings,*
*Now for October eves!*

**—Humbert Wolfe**

❍❖❍

*How beautiful is the rain!*
*After the dust and heat,*
*In the broad and fiery street,*
*In the narrow lane,*
*How beautiful is the rain!*

**—Henry Wadsworth Longfellow**

❍❖❍

Everywhere water is a thing of beauty
Gleaming in the dewdrop,
Singing in the summer rain.

**—John Ballantine Gough**

❍❖❍

*No spring nor summer beauty hath such grace,*
*As I have seen in one autumnal face.*

**—John Donne**

❍❖❍

Summer is delicious, rain is refreshing, wind braces up, snow is exhilarating; there is no such thing as bad weather, only different kinds of good weather.

**—John Ruskin**

❍❖❍

Indoors or out, no one relaxes in March, that month of wind and taxes, the wind will presently disappear, the taxes last us all the year.

**—Ogden Nash**

❍❖❍

*The air is like a butterfly,*
*With frail blue wings.*
*The happy earth looks at the sky,*
*And sings.*

**—Joyce Kilmer**

❍❖❍

*Come, fill the cup, and in the fire of spring,*
*The winter garment of repentance fling:*
*The bird of time has but a little way*
*To fly – and lo! The bird is on the wing.*

**—Omar Khayyám**

❍❖❍

*The year's at spring*
*And day's at morn;*
*God's in his heaven,*
*All's right with the world.*

**—Robert Browning**

❍❖❍

*I sing of brooks, of blossoms, birds, and bowers:*
*Of April, May, of June, and July flowers.*
*I sing of maypoles, hock-carts, wassails, wakes,*
*Of bridegrooms, brides, and of their bridal cakes.*

**—Robert Herrick**

❍❖❍

October's poplars are flaming torches lighting the way to winter.

**—Nova Bair**

❍❖❍

Youth is like spring, an over-praised season more remarkable for biting winds than genial breezes. Autumn is the mellower season, and what we lose in flowers, we more than gain in fruits.

**—Samuel Butler**

❍❖❍

*Spring, the sweet spring, is the year's pleasant king;*
*Then blooms each thing, then maids dance in a ring,*
*Cold doth not sting, the pretty birds do sing.*
*Cuckoo, jug-jug, pu-we, to-witta-woo!*

**—Thomas Nash**

❍❖❍

*April is the cruellest month, breeding*
*Lilacs out of the dead land, mixing*
*Memory and desire, stirring*
*Dull roots with spring rain.*

**—TS Eliot**

- *Watch the snowflakes as they fall,*
  *Try so hard to count them all.*
  *Build a snowman way up high—*
  *See if he can touch the sky.*
  *Snow forts, snowballs, angels, too,*
  *In the snow, so white and new.*
  *Slip and slide and skate so fast.*
  *Wintertime is here at last.*

- *Spring is not the best of seasons.*
  *Cold and flu are two good reasons;*
  *Wind and rain and other sorrow,*
  *Warm today and cold tomorrow.*
  *Whoever said spring was romantic?*
  *The word that best applies is frantic!*

- *The earth is warm, the sun's ablaze,*
  *It is a time of carefree days;*
  *And bees abuzz that chance to pass*
  *May see me snoozing on the grass.*

**—Anonymous**

## Charming Smiles

A smile is a curve that sets everything straight.

**—Phyllis Diller**

❍❖❍

A smile is the light in your window that tells others that there is a caring, sharing person inside.

**—Denis Waitley**

❍❖❍

- He who smiles rather than rages is always the stronger.
- Never rely on the glory of the morning, nor the smiles of your mother-in-law.

**—Japanese Proverb**

❍❖❍

A smile abroad is often a scowl at home.

**—Lord Alfred Tennyson**

❍❖❍

Smiles form the channel of a future tear.

**—Lord Byron**

❍❖❍

*No matter how grouchy you're feeling*
*You'll find the smile more or less healing.*
*It grows in a wreath*
*All around the front teeth—*
*Thus preserving the face from congealing.*

**—Anthony Euwer**

❍❖❍

Wrinkles should merely indicate where smiles have been.

**—Mark Twain**

❍❖❍

Smile more often! Give someone a hug! Praise someone for doing a job well done! These are the little things that can make a big difference in a person's life. Do you notice that they are all free? They are free to give and free to receive. This just gives you another reason to SMILE, hug and praise more!

**—Mary Shaw**

❍❖❍

There are many kinds of smiles, each having a distinct character. Some announce goodness and sweetness, others betray sarcasm, bitterness and pride; some soften the countenance by their languishing tenderness, others brighten by their spiritual vivacity.

**—Johann Kaspar Lavater**

❍❖❍

If you smile when no one else is around, you really mean it.

**—Andy Rooney**

❍❖❍

- Peace begins with a smile.
- Let us always meet each other with a smile, for the smile is the beginning of love.
- Smile at each other, smile at your wife, smile at your husband, smile at your children – it doesn't matter who it is – and that will help you to grow up in greater love for each other.

**—Mother Teresa**

❍❖❍

Beauty is truth's smile when she beholds her own face in a perfect mirror.

**—Rabindranath Tagore**

❍❖❍

The warmth of a smile can light up a person's day.

**—Rabbi Moshe Goldberger**

❍❖❍

Start every day with a smile and get it over with.

**—WC Fields**

❍❖❍

- The world always looks brighter from behind a smile.
- My heart smiled when you kissed my lips. What a sweet surprise.
- Laugh when you're winning and smile when you're down.
- Smiles never go up in price or down in value.
- A smile is the heart's way of breathing.
- Love begins with a smile, grows with a kiss, and ends with a teardrop.
- It takes 26 muscles to smile, but 62 muscles to frown.
- Smiles are free – don't save them.
- Smile and the world smiles with you. Cry and you cry alone.
- A winning smile makes winners of us all.
- Don't frown. You never know who is falling in love with your smile.
- So many languages in the world and a smile speaks them all.
- Never stop smiling, because you know that if the eyes are the window to the soul, then the smile is the front door.
- When there are lines upon my face from a lifetime of smiles, when the time comes to embrace for one long last while, we can laugh about how time really flies, we won't say goodbye, cause true love never dies. You'll always be beautiful in my eyes.
- A smile costs nothing but gives much. It enriches those who receive without making poorer those who give. It takes but a moment, but the memory of it sometimes lasts forever. None is so rich or mighty that he cannot get along without it and none is so poor that he cannot be made rich by it. Yet a smile cannot be bought, begged, borrowed, or stolen, for it is something that is of no value to anyone until it is given away. Some people are too tired to give you a smile. Give them one of yours, as none needs a smile so much as he who has no more to give.

**—Anonymous**

○❖○

There's a smile in my heart that I've waited my whole life for.

**—Shyla**

○❖○

*There was a young lady of Riga,*
*Who rode with a smile on a tiger;*
*They returned from the ride,*
*With the lady inside,*
*And the smile on the face of the tiger.*

**—Langford Reed**

❍❖❍

The world is like a mirror, you see? Smile, and your friends smile back.

**—Zen Saying**

❍❖❍

I love the man that can smile in trouble – that can gather strength from distress, and grow brave by reflection. 'Tis the business of little minds to shrink, but he whose heart is firm, and whose conscience approves his conduct, will pursue his principles unto death.

**—Thomas Paine**

❍❖❍

A warm smile is the universal language of kindness.

**—William Arthur Ward**

# The Essence of Happiness

Most people are about as happy as they make up their minds to be.

**—Abraham Lincoln**

- To live happily is an inward power of the soul.
- Happiness is an expression of the soul in considered actions.
- Happiness depends upon ourselves.
- People of superior refinement and active disposition identify happiness with honour; for this is, roughly speaking, the end of political life.

**—Aristotle**

The greatest essentials of happiness are something to do, someone to love, and something to hope for.

**—Allan K Chalmers**

Thousands of candles can be lit from a single candle, and the life of the candle will not be shortened. Happiness never decreases by being shared.

**—Buddha**

Happiness: We rarely feel it.  
I would buy it, beg it, steal it,  
Pay in coins of dripping blood  
For this one transcendent good.

**—Amy Lowell**

- Man needs, for his happiness, not only the enjoyment of this or that, but hope and enterprise and change.
- If all our happiness is bound up entirely in our personal circumstances, it is difficult not to demand of life more than it has to give.
- If there were in the world today any large number of people who desired their own happiness more than they desired the unhappiness of others, we could have paradise in a few years.

**—Bertrand Russell**

❍❖❍

Action may not always bring happiness; but there is no happiness without action.

**—Benjamin Disraeli**

❍❖❍

Happiness is like a kiss. You must share it to enjoy it.

**—Bernard Meltzer**

❍❖❍

- The Constitution only guarantees the American people the right to pursue happiness. You have to catch it yourself.
- There are two ways of being happy: we must either diminish our wants or augment our means – either may do – the result is the same and it is for each man to decide for himself and to do that which happens to be easier.

**—Benjamin Franklin**

❍❖❍

Happiness is not a destination. It is a method of life.

**—Burton Hills**

❍❖❍

- Happiness is like a sunbeam, which the least shadow intercepts.
- If you want happiness for an hour, take a nap.  
If you want happiness for a day, go fishing.  
If you want happiness for a year, inherit a fortune.  
If you want happiness for a lifetime, help somebody.

**—Chinese Proverb**

❍❖❍

The happiness of life is made up of minute fractions – the little, soon-forgotten charities of a kiss, a smile, a kind look, a heartfelt compliment in the disguise of a playful raillery.

**—Coleridge**

❍❖❍

Happiness is not easily won; it is hard to find it in ourselves, and impossible to find it elsewhere.

**—Chamfort**

❍❖❍

Happiness, that grand mistress of the ceremonies in the dance of life, impels us through all its mazes and meanderings, but leads none of us by the same route.

**—Charles Caleb Colton**

❍❖❍

If you want others to be happy, practise compassion. If you want to be happy, practise compassion.

**—Dalai Lama**

❍❖❍

Happiness is different from pleasure. Happiness has something to do with struggling, enduring and accomplishing.

**—George Sheehan**

❍❖❍

Happiness is the interval between periods of unhappiness.

**—Don Marquis**

❍❖❍

Happiness doesn't depend on outward conditions. It depends on inner conditions. It isn't what you have or who you are or where you are or what you are doing that makes you happy or unhappy. It is what you think about it.

**—Dale Carnegie**

❍❖❍

Happiness in intelligent people is the rarest thing I know.

**—Ernest Hemingway**

❍❖❍

Happiness is not a goal; it is a by-product.

**—Eleanor Roosevelt**

❍❖❍

Happiness is a positive cash flow.

**—Fred Adler**

❍❖❍

Whether happiness may come or not, one should try and prepare oneself to do without it.

**—George Eliot**

❍❖❍

I, not events, have the power to make me happy or unhappy today. I can choose which it shall be. Yesterday is dead, tomorrow hasn't arrived yet. I have just one day, today, and I'm going to be happy in it.

**—Groucho Marx**

❍❖❍

True happiness is not attained through self-gratification but through fidelity to a worthy purpose.

**—Helen Keller**

❍❖❍

I have no money, no resources, no hopes. I am the happiest man alive.

**—Henry Miller**

❍❖❍

Happiness requires problems.

**—HL Hollingworth**

❍❖❍

He's happy who, far away from business, like the races of men of old, tills his ancestral fields with his own oxen, unbound by any interest to pay.

**—Horace**

❍❖❍

Success is getting what you want. Happiness is liking what you get.

**—H Jackson Brown**

❍❖❍

Happiness is a matter of one's most ordinary and everyday mode of consciousness being busy and lively and unconcerned with self.

**—Iris Murdoch**

❍❖❍

Everyone wants happiness, no one wants pain, but you can't make a rainbow without a little rain.

**—Idk**

❍❖❍

Happiness is like a butterfly which, when pursued, is always beyond our grasp, but which, if you will sit down quietly, may alight upon you.

**—Nathaniel Hawthorne**

❍❖❍

Happiness comes more from loving than being loved, and often when our affection seems wounded, it is only our vanity bleeding. To love, and to be hurt often, and to love again – this is the brave and happy life.

**—JE Buckrose**

❍❖❍

We must laugh before we are happy, for fear we die before we laugh at all.

**—Jean de La Bruyere**

❍❖❍

Happiness comes when we test our skills towards some meaningful purpose.

**—John Stossel**

❍❖❍

Do good, and you will find that happiness will run after you.

**—James Freeman Clarke**

❍❖❍

The foolish man seeks happiness in the distance; the wise man grows it under his feet.

**—James Oppenheim**

❍❖❍

Three grand essentials to happiness in this life are something to do, something to love and something to hope for.

**—Joseph Addison**

❍❖❍

Happiness is a conscious choice, not an automatic response.

**—Mildred Barthel**

❍❖❍

Happiness and virtue react upon each other – the best are not only the happiest, but the happiest are usually the best.

**—Lytton**

❍❖❍

There are people who can do all fine and heroic things but one – keep from telling their happiness to the unhappy.

**—Mark Twain**

❍❖❍

A major cause of unhappiness is overestimating the happiness of others.

**—Margaret Thomas**

❍❖❍

Happiness is having a scratch for every itch...

**—Ogden Nash**

❍❖❍

One of the keys to happiness is a bad memory.

**—Rita Mae Brown**

❍❖❍

Remember that happiness is a way of travel – not a destination.

**—Roy M Goodman**

❍❖❍

- Nothing can bring you happiness but yourself.
- Happiness is a perfume you cannot pour on others without getting a few drops on yourself.

**—Ralph Waldo Emerson**

❍❖❍

You needn't tell me that a man who doesn't love oysters and asparagus and good wines has got a soul, or a stomach either. He's simply got the instinct for being unhappy.

**—Saki**

❍❖❍

Happiness is an imaginary condition, formerly often attributed to the dead, now usually attributed by adults to children, and by children to adults.

**—Thomas Szasz**

❍❖❍

Happiness makes up in height for what it lacks in length.

**—Robert Frost**

❍❖❍

Real happiness is cheap enough, yet how deeply we pay for its counterfeit.

**—Hosea Ballou**

❍❖❍

Happiness is like a cat. If you try to coax it or call it, it will avoid you; it will never come. But if you pay not attention to it and go about your business, you'll find it rubbing against your legs and jumping into your lap.

**—William Bennett**

❍❖❍

- I asked for riches, that I might be happy. I was given poverty, that I might be wise.
- Happy memories never wear out. Relive them as often as you want.
- Like swimming, riding, writing or playing golf, happiness can be learned.
- Happiness is enhanced by others but does not depend upon others.
- Love means making the other happy, even from a distance.
- The happiest of people don't necessarily have the best of everything; they just make the most of everything that comes along their way.
- Forbidden love provides happiness when there is no happiness.
- Happiness is the feeling you're feeling when you want to keep feeling it.
- The secret to happiness is not in doing what one likes to do, but in liking what one has to do.
- Not only is there a right to be happy, there is a duty to be happy. So much sadness exists in the world that we are all under obligation to contribute as much joy as lies within our powers.

**—Anonymous**

The greatest happiness of life is the conviction that we are loved – loved for ourselves, or rather, loved in spite of ourselves.

**—Victor Hugo**

❍❖❍

Happiness is essentially a state of going somewhere, one directionally, without regret or reservation.

**—William H Sheldon**

❍❖❍

The greatest happiness you can have is knowing that you do not necessarily require happiness.

**—William Saroyan**

❍❖❍

When a small child, I thought that success spelled happiness. I was wrong – happiness is like a butterfly, which appears and delights us for one brief moment, but soon flits away.

**—Anna Pavlova**

# Musical Notes

All music is folk music. I ain't never heard no horse sing a song.

**—Louis Armstrong**

❍❖❍

Wagner's music is better than it sounds.

**—Mark Twain**

❍❖❍

I may not be a first-class composer, but I am a first-class second-rate composer.

**—Richard Strauss**

❍❖❍

After silence, that which comes nearest to expressing the inexpressible is music.

**—Aldous Huxley**

❍❖❍

The notes I handle no better than many pianists. But the pauses between the notes – ah, that is where the art resides.

**—Arthur Schnabel**

❍❖❍

There is no doubt that the first requirement for a composer is to be dead.

**—Arthur Honegger**

❍❖❍

Music washes away from the soul the dust of everyday life.

**—Berthold Auerbach**

❍❖❍

It is cruel, you know, that music should be so beautiful. It has the beauty of loneliness and of pain: of strength and freedom. The beauty of disappointment and never-satisfied love. The cruel beauty of nature and the everlasting beauty of monotony.

**—Benjamin Britten**

❍❖❍

Music is the silence between the notes.

**—Claude Debussy**

❍❖❍

Nothing separates the generations more than music. By the time a child is eight or nine, he has developed a passion for his own music that is even stronger than his passion for procrastination and weird clothes.

**—Bill Cosby**

❍❖❍

Music is good to the melancholy, bad to those who mourn, and neither good nor bad to the deaf.

**—Benedict Spinoza**

❍❖❍

One good thing about music... when it hits you feel no pain... so hit me with music.

**—Bob Marley**

❍❖❍

Music has been called the speech of the angels; I will go further and call it the speech of God himself.

**—Charles Kingsley**

❍❖❍

- Only sick music makes money today.
- Without music, life would be an error. The German imagines even God singing songs.

**—Friedrich Nietzsche**

❍❖❍

The whole business is built on ego, vanity, self-satisfaction, and it's total crap to pretend it's not.

**—George Michael**

❍❖❍

- Music, in performance, is a type of sculpture. The air in the performance is sculpted into something.
- All the good music has already been written by people with wigs and stuff.

**—Frank Zappa**

❍❖❍

I think I should have no other mortal wants, if I could always have plenty of music. It seems to infuse strength into my limbs and ideas into my brain. Life seems to go on without effort, when I am filled with music.

**—George Eliot**

❍❖❍

Give me a laundry list and I'll set it to music.

**—Gioacchino Antonio Rossini**

❍❖❍

Hell is full of musical amateurs: music is the brandy of the damned.

**—George Bernard Shaw**

❍❖❍

Music stands halfway between thought and phenomenon, between spirit and matter, a sort of nebulous mediator, like and unlike the things it mediates.

**—Heinrich Heine**

❍❖❍

Music is the universal language of mankind – poetry their universal pastime and delight.

**—Henry Wadsworth Longfellow**

❍❖❍

Music must take rank as the highest of the fine arts – as the one which, more than any other, ministers to human welfare.

**—Herbert Spencer**

❍❖❍

- A good composer does not imitate; he steals.
- Too many pieces of music finish too long after the end.

**—Igor Stravinsky**

❍❖❍

Heard melodies are sweet, but those unheard are sweeter.

**—John Keats**

❍❖❍

Music is an indirect force for change, because it provides an anchor against human tragedy.

**—Jessie Michael**

❍❖❍

Music is the poetry of the air.

**—Jean Paul Richter**

❍❖❍

Music has charms to soothe a savage breast, to soften rocks, or bend a knotted oak.

**—William Congreve**

❍❖❍

Musicians talk of nothing but money and jobs. Give me businessmen every time. They really are interested in music and art.

**—Jean Sibelius**

❍❖❍

- Music is a higher revelation than philosophy.
- Music should strike fire from the heart of man, and bring tears from the eyes of woman.
- Beethoven can write music, thank God, but he can do nothing else on earth.

**—Ludwig van Beethoven**

❍❖❍

I have no pleasure in any man who despises music. It is no invention of ours: it is a gift of God. I place it next to theology. Satan hates music: he knows how it drives the evil spirit out of us.

**—Martin Luther**

❍❖❍

Life is about the betterment of the human condition, stretching one's own mind, increasing social awareness, or even random acts of kindness that spill into the soul of humanity. This is why I play music.

**—Mark Haugh**

❍❖❍

Music makes one feel so romantic – at least it always gets on one's nerves – which is the same thing nowadays.

**—Oscar Wilde**

❍❖❍

Take a music bath once or twice a week for a few seasons, and you will find that it is to the soul what the water-bath is to the body.

**—Oliver Wendell Holmes**

❍❖❍

As long as there are kids who are pissed off and have no real way in venting out that anger, heavy metal will live on.

**—Ozzy Osborne**

❍❖❍

Compare music to drinks. Some is like a strong brandy. Some is like a fine wine. The music you're playing sounds like Diet Coke.

**—Pavarotti**

❍❖❍

The introduction of a new kind of music must be shunned as imperilling the whole state, since styles of music are never disturbed without affecting the most important political institutions.

**—Plato**

❍❖❍

Music is the wine that fills the cup of silence.

**—Robert Fripp**

❍❖❍

There are two golden rules for an orchestra: start together and finish together. The public doesn't give a damn what goes on in between.

**—Sir Thomas Beecham**

❍❖❍

Music expresses that which, if music be the food of love, play on.

**—William Shakespeare**

❍❖❍

*Music, when soft voices die,*
*Vibrates in the memory.*

**—Percy B Shelly**

❍❖❍

Music is well said to be the speech of angels; in fact, nothing among the utterances allowed to man is felt to be so divine. It brings us near to the Infinite.

**—Thomas Carlyle**

❍❖❍

The world speaks to me in pictures, my soul answers in music.

**—Rabindranath Tagore**

❍❖❍

Life can't be all bad when, for ten dollars, you can buy all the Beethoven sonatas and listen to them for ten years.

**—William F Buckley, Jr**

Music knows no country, race or creed;
But gives to each according to his need.

**—Anonymous**

# MAN AND ANIMAL

I am not a vegetarian because I love animals; I am a vegetarian because I hate plants.

**—A Whitney Brown**

Man can soar higher than angels; he can sink lower than beasts.

**—Zarathushtra**

- Anyone who has accustomed himself to regard the life of any living creature as worthless is in danger of arriving also at the idea of worthless human lives.
- We must fight against the spirit of unconscious cruelty with which we treat the animals. Animals suffer as much as we do. True humanity does not allow us to impose such sufferings on them. It is our duty to make the whole world recognise it.

**—Albert Schweitzer**

You become responsible forever for what you have tamed.

**—Antoine de Saint-Exupery**

- I am in favour of animal rights as well as human rights. That is the way of a whole human being.
- I care not for a man's religion whose dog and cat are not the better for it.

**—Abraham Lincoln**

❍❖❍

The animals of the world exist for their own reasons. They were not made for humans any more than black people were made for white, or women created for men.

**—Alice Walker**

❍❖❍

The indifference, callousness and contempt that so many people exhibit towards animals is evil first because it results in great suffering in animals, and second because it results in an incalculably great impoverishment of the human spirit.

**—Ashley Montagu**

❍❖❍

I guess cows aren't into the four food groups, especially when they are two of them.

**—Anthony Clark**

❍❖❍

Man is an animal which, alone among the animals, refuses to be satisfied by the fulfilment of animal desires.

**—Alexander Graham Bell**

❍❖❍

At his best, man is the noblest of all animals; separated from law and justice, he is the worst.

**—Aristotle**

❍❖❍

Man is an animal that makes bargains; no other animal does this – one dog does not change a bone with another.

**—Adam Smith**

❍❖❍

The key to everything is patience. You get the chicken by hatching the egg – not by smashing it.

**—Arnold Glasgow**

❍❖❍

Our task must be to free ourselves... by widening our circle of compassion to embrace all living creatures and the whole of nature and its beauty.

**—Albert Einstein**

❍❖❍

If not to steal food, would a cat go up on the counter? Why did George Mallory try to go up on Mount Everest, which was quite a lot more trouble? Because it is there...

**—Barbara Holland**

❍❖❍

Teaching a child not to step on a caterpillar is as valuable to the child as it is to the caterpillar.

**—Bradley Miller**

❍❖❍

Our land is more valuable than your money. As long as the sun shines and the waters flow, this land will be here to give life to men and animals; therefore, we cannot sell this land. It was put here for us by the Great Spirit and we cannot sell it because it does not belong to us.

**—Blackfoot Chief**

❍❖❍

He was so learned that he could name a horse in nine languages; so ignorant that he bought a cow to ride on.

**—Benjamin Franklin**

❍❖❍

There is no psychiatrist in the world like a puppy licking your face.

**—Ben Williams**

❍❖❍

Though boys throw stones at frogs in sport, the frogs do not die in sport but in earnest.

**—Bion**

The person who kills for fun is announcing that, could he get away with it, he'd kill you for fun. Your life may be of no consequence to anyone else but is invaluable to you because it's the only one you've got. Exactly the same is true of each individual deer, hare, rabbit, fox, fish, pheasant and butterfly. Humans should enjoy their own lives, not taking others'.

**—Brigid Brophy**

Flatterers look like friends, as wolves like dogs.

**—George Chapman**

❍❖❍

Authors are sometimes like tomcats: They distrust all the other toms but they are kind to kittens.

**—Malcolm Cowley**

❍❖❍

The eating of meat extinguishes the seed of great compassion.

**—Buddha**

❍❖❍

We must educate the public. The average person has no idea of what's going on in factory farms, in laboratories, circuses, roadside zoos or rodeos.

**—Bob Barker**

❍❖❍

Animals, whom we have made our slaves, we do not like to consider our equals.

**—Charles Darwin**

❍❖❍

If I die before my cat, I want a little of my ashes put in his food so I can live inside him.

**—Drew Barrymore**

❍❖❍

Life is as dear to a mute creature as it is to man. Just as one wants happiness and fears pain, just as one wants to live and not die, so do other creatures.

**—Dalai Lama**

❍❖❍

Pain is pain, whether it be inflicted on man or on beast; and the creature who suffers it, whether man or beast, being sensible to the misery of it, whilst it lasts, suffers evil. The white man can have no right, by virtue of his colour, to enslave and tyrannize over a black man. For the same reason, a man can have no natural right to abuse and torment a beast.

**—Dr Humphrey Primatt**

❍❖❍

Many times I am asked why the suffering of animals should call forth more sympathy from me than the suffering of human beings. My answer is that because I believe that this work includes all the education and lines of reform, which are needed to make a perfect circle of peace and goodwill about the earth.

**—Ella Wheeler Wilcox**

❍❖❍

It is an important fact that things are not always what they seem. For instance, man had always assumed that he was more intelligent than dolphins because he had achieved so much – the wheel, New York, wars and so on – whilst all the dolphins had ever done was muck about in the water having a good time. But conversely, the dolphins had always believed that they were far more intelligent than man – for precisely the same reasons.

**—Douglas Adams**

❍❖❍

Wild animals never kill for sport. Man is the only one to whom the torture and death of his fellow creatures is amusing in itself.

**—Froude**

❍❖❍

The fate of animals is of greater importance to me than the fear of appearing ridiculous; it is indissolubly connected with the fate of man.

**—Emile Zola**

❍❖❍

I used to look at [my dog] Smokey and think, 'If you were a little smarter you could tell me what you were thinking,' and he'd look at me like he was saying, 'If you were a little smarter, I wouldn't have to.'

**—Fred Jungclaus**

❍❖❍

If you have men who will exclude any of God's creatures from the shelter of compassion and pity, you will have men who will deal likewise with their fellow men.

**—St. Francis of Assisi**

❍❖❍

When a man's best friend is his dog, that dog has a problem.

**—Edward Abbey**

❍❖❍

Animals in different countries have different expressions, just as the people in different countries differ in expression.

**—Gertrude Stein**

❍❖❍

The greatness of a nation and its moral progress can be judged by the way its animals are treated... I hold that, the more helpless a creature, the more entitled it is to protection by man from the cruelty of man.

**—Mahatma Gandhi**

❍❖❍

When a man wants to murder a tiger, it's called sport. When the tiger wants to murder him, it's called ferocity.

**—George Bernard Shaw**

❍❖❍

He is my other eyes that can see above the clouds, my other ears that hear above the winds. He is the part of me that can reach out into the sea. He has told me a thousand times over that I am his reason for being; by the way he rests against my leg; by the way he thumps his tail at my smallest smile; by the way he shows his hurt when I leave without taking him. (I think it makes him sick with worry when he is not along to care for me.)

**—Gene Hill**

I have no doubt that it is a part of the destiny of the human race, in its gradual improvement, to leave off eating animals, as surely as the savage tribes have left off eating each other when they came in contact with the more civilised.

**—Henry David Thoreau**

Men are the only animals that devote themselves, day in and day out, to making one another unhappy. It is an art like any other. Its virtuosi are called altruists.

**—HL Mencken**

People often say that humans have always eaten animals, as if this is a justification for continuing the practice. According to this logic, we should not try to prevent people from murdering other people, since this has also been done since the earliest of times.

**—Isaac Singer**

❍❖❍

Every man is sociable until a cow invades his garden.

**—Irish Proverb**

❍❖❍

- If a man earnestly seeks a righteous life, his first act of abstinence is from animal food...
- A human can be healthy without killing animals for food. Therefore if he eats meat he participates in taking animal life merely for the sake of his appetite. Man, by violating his own feelings, becomes cruel. And how deeply seated in the human heart is the injunction not to take life.

**—Leo Tolstoy**

❍❖❍

- Man is the only animal that blushes – or needs to.
- Of all the creatures ever made, man is the most detestable. Of the entire brood, he is the only one that possesses malice. He is the only creature that inflicts pain for sport, knowing it to be pain.
- I am not interested to know whether vivisection produces results that are profitable to the human race or not.... The pain it inflicts upon unconsenting animals is the basis of my enmity towards it, and it is to me sufficient justification for the enmity without looking further.

**—Mark Twain**

❍❖❍

Some people are uncomfortable with the idea that humans belong to the same class of animals as cats and cows and raccoons. They're like the people who become successful and then don't want to be reminded of the old neighbourhood.

**—Phil Donahue**

❍❖❍

For as long as man continues to be the ruthless destroyer of lower living beings, he will never know health or peace. For as long as men massacre animals, they will kill each other. Indeed, he who sows the seeds of murder and pain cannot reap joy and love.

**—Pythagoras**

❍❖❍

The difference between man and animals is that we don't use our tongue to clean our genitals.

**—Rimmer**

❍❖❍

If a man wants to be of the greatest possible value to his fellow creatures, let him begin the long, solitary task of perfecting himself.

**—Robertson Davies**

❍❖❍

This is what you should do: love the earth and sun and the animals, despise riches, give alms to everyone that asks, stand up for the stupid and crazy, devote your income and labour to others, hate tyrants, argue not concerning God, have patience and indulgence towards the people.... re-examine all you have been told at school or church or in any book, dismiss what insults your own soul, and your very flesh shall be a great poem.

**—Walt Whitman**

❍❖❍

Man is the only animal that laughs and weeps, for he is the only animal that is struck with the difference between what things are and what they ought to be.

**—William Hazlitt**

❍❖❍

There is an Indian legend which says when a human dies there is a bridge they must cross to enter into heaven. At the head of that bridge waits every animal that humans encountered during their lifetime. The animals, based upon what they know of this person, decide which humans may cross the bridge.... and which are turned away....

**—Anonymous**

## Feminine Talk

When women go wrong, men go right after them.

**—Mae West**

❍❖❍

You don't know a woman until you have had a letter from her.

**—Ada Leverson**

❍❖❍

Give a girl the correct footwear and she can conquer the world.

**—Bette Midler**

❍❖❍

One should never trust a woman who tells one her real age. A woman who would tell one that, would tell one anything.

**—Oscar Wilde**

❍❖❍

God gave women intuition and femininity. Used properly, the combination easily jumbles the brain of any man I've ever met.

**—Farrah Fawcett**

❍❖❍

- In my heart, I think a woman has two choices: either she's a feminist or a masochist.
- A woman without a man is like a fish without a bicycle.

**—Gloria Steinem**

❍❖❍

There are worse occupations in this world than feeling a woman's pulse.

**—Laurence Sterne**

❍❖❍

When women are the advisers, the lords of creation don't take the advice till they have persuaded themselves that it is just what they intended to do. Then they act upon it, and if it succeeds, they give the weaker vessel half the credit for it; if it fails, they generously give her the whole.

**—Louisa May Alcott**

❍❖❍

Because I am a woman, I must make unusual efforts to succeed. If I fail, no one will say, "She doesn't have what it takes." They will say, "Women don't have what it takes."

**—Clare Boothe Luce**

❍❖❍

All women are parts of the Divine Mother and, therefore, they should be looked upon as mothers by all.

**—Sri Ramakrishna**

❍❖❍

From birth to 18, a girl needs good parents; from 18 to 35, she needs good looks; from 35 to 55, good personality; from 55 on, she needs good cash. I'm saving my money.

**—Sophie Tucker**

❍❖❍

As a woman I have no country. As a woman my country is the whole world.

**—Virginia Woolf**

❍❖❍

Women are like elephants. I like to watch them, but I wouldn't want to own one.

**—WC Fields**

❍❖❍

Woman is the teacher of gentility to man. She helps man to grow in moral height. She is the sustaining power of life of man.

**—Zarathushtra**

❍❖❍

Girls are like phones – they like to be held tight and talked to, but if you push the wrong button you'll be disconnected!

**—Anonymous**

# Man Talk, Woman Talk

God help the man who won't marry until he finds a perfect woman, and God help him still more if he finds her.

**—Benjamin Tillett**

- A man can be happy with any woman as long as he does not love her.
- All women become like their mothers. That is their tragedy. No man does. That is his.
- The English country gentleman galloping after a fox – the unspeakable in full pursuit of the uneatable.

**—Oscar Wilde**

A ship is always referred to as "she" because it costs so much to keep one in paint and powder.

**—Chester Nimitz**

A diplomat is a man who always remembers a woman's birthday but never remembers her age.

**—Robert Frost**

A man must marry only a very pretty woman in case he should ever want some other man to take her off his hands.

**—Sacha Guitry**

# Life Speak

- There are two ways to live your life. One is as though nothing is a miracle. The other is as though everything is a miracle.
- True religion is real living; living with all one's soul, with all one's goodness and righteousness.

**—Albert Einstein**

❍❖❍

Three passions have governed my life: The longings for love, the search for knowledge, and unbearable pity for the suffering of humankind.

**—Bertrand Russell**

❍❖❍

Life's tragedy is that we get old too soon and wise too late.

**—Benjamin Franklin**

❍❖❍

- Just as a candle cannot burn without fire, men cannot live without a spiritual life.
- On life's journey faith is nourishment, virtuous deeds are a shelter, wisdom is the light by day and right-mindfulness is the protection by night. If a man lives a pure life, nothing can destroy him.

**—Buddha**

❍❖❍

If you enjoy what you do, you'll never work another day in your life.

**—Confucius**

❍❖❍

Life is too important to take seriously.

**—Corky Siegel**

❍❖❍

The people whom I have seen succeed best in life have always been cheerful and hopeful, who went about their business with a smile on their faces, and took the changes and chances of this mortal life with strength, facing rough and smooth alike as it came.

**—Charles Kingsley**

❍❖❍

The purpose of life is to fight maturity.

**—Dick Werthimer**

❍❖❍

Love is anterior to Life
Posterior to Death
Initial of Creation, and
The exponent of Earth.

**—Emily Dickinson**

❍❖❍

We are sinful not merely because we have eaten of the tree of knowledge, but also because we have not eaten of the tree of life.

**—Franz Kafka**

❍❖❍

Life is no brief candle to me. It is a sort of splendid torch, which I have got hold of for the moment, and I want to make it burn as brightly as possible before handing it on to future generations.

**—George Bernard Shaw**

❍❖❍

Life is half spent before we know what it is.

**—George Herbert**

❍❖❍

Life is a great big canvas, and you should throw all the paint on it you can.

**—Danny Kaye**

❍❖❍

A useless life is an early death.

**—Goethe**

❍❖❍

Develop an interest in life as you see it; the people, things, literature, music – the world is so rich, simply throbbing with rich treasures, beautiful souls and interesting people. Forget yourself.

**—Henry Miller**

❍❖❍

When I realised – with certainty and no equivocation – that a toothache caused me more agony than all the wretchedness and misery of Africa and Asia, I resolved to give up worrying my head about man's destiny and to see my dentist more often.

**—Irving Layton**

❍❖❍

There is no wealth but life.

**—John Ruskin**

❍❖❍

Life is what happens to you while you're busy making other plans.

**—John Lennon**

❍❖❍

Love is life and if you miss love, you miss life.

**—Leo Buscaglia**

❍❖❍

Good friends, good books and a sleepy conscience: this is the ideal life.

**—Mark Twain**

❍❖❍

Life is a promise; fulfil it.

**—Mother Teresa**

❍❖❍

If you have known how to compose your life, you have done a great deal more than the person who knows how to compose a book. You have done more than the one who has taken cities and empires.

**—Michel de Montaigne**

❍❖❍

My life is my message.

**—Mahatma Gandhi**

❍❖❍

Life is one fool thing after another, whereas love is two fool things after each other.

**—Oscar Wilde**

❍❖❍

The life that is unexamined is not worth living.

**—Plato**

❍❖❍

Taking joy in life is a woman's best cosmetic.

**—Rosalind Russell**

❍❖❍

Life is short, but its ills make it seem long.

**—Publius Syrus**

❍❖❍

Life can only be understood backwards; but it must be lived forwards.

**—Soren Aabye Kierkegaard**

❍❖❍

No man enjoys the true taste of life, but he who is ready and willing to quit it.

**—Seneca**

❍❖❍

Many of life's failures are people who did not realise how close they were to success when they gave up.

**—Thomas Edison**

❍❖❍

Not life, but good life, is to be chiefly valued.

**—Socrates**

❍❖❍

Life is a song – sing it.
Life is a game – play it.
Life is a challenge – meet it.
Life is a dream – realise it.
Life is a sacrifice – offer it.
Life is love – enjoy it.

**—Sai Baba**

❍❖❍

Each day is a little life.

**—Arthur Schopenhauer**

❍❖❍

I have measured out my life with coffee spoons.

**—TS Eliot**

❍❖❍

We make a living by what we get, we make a life by what we give.

**—Winston Churchill**

❍❖❍

No man is a failure who is enjoying life.

**—William Feather**

❍❖❍

We cannot do great things – only small things with great love.

**—Mother Teresa**

❍❖❍

It's just a job. Grass grows, birds fly, waves pound the sand. I beat people up.

**—Muhammad Ali**

❍❖❍

- Life is a song. Love is the music.
- Learn from yesterday, live for today, hope for tomorrow.
- Human life is purely a matter of deciding what's important to you.
- Life is like a beautiful melody; only the lyrics are messed up.

**—Anonymous**

# Garden Wisdom

The way of cultivation is not easy.
He who plants a garden plants happiness.

**—Chinese Proverb**

❍❖❍

Gardening is the purest of human pleasures.

**—Francis Bacon**

❍❖❍

There is a garden in every childhood, an enchanted place where colours are brighter, the air softer, and the morning more fragrant than ever again.

**—Elizabeth Lawrence**

❍❖❍

The garden is the poor man's apothecary.

**—German Proverb**

❍❖❍

Gardens.... should be like lovely, well-shaped girls: all curves, secret corners, unexpected deviations, seductive surprises and then still more curves.

**—HE Bates**

❍❖❍

The world is so empty if one thinks only of mountains, rivers, and cities; but to know someone here and there who thinks and feels with us and though distant, is close to us in spirit – this makes the earth for us an inhabited garden.

**—Johann von Goethe**

❍❖❍

No two gardens are the same. No two days are the same in one garden.

**—Hugh Johnson**

❍❖❍

The poetry of the earth is never dead.

**—John Keats**

❍❖❍

Gardening is a kind of disease. It infects you; you cannot escape it. When you go visiting, your eyes rove about the garden; you interrupt the serious cocktail drinking because of an irresistible impulse to get up and pull a weed.

**—Lewis Gannit**

Weather means more when you have a garden. There's nothing like listening to a shower and thinking how it is soaking in around your green beans.

**—Marcelene Cox**

*Kind hearts are the gardens,*
*Kind thoughts are the roots,*
*Kind words are the flowers,*
*Kind deeds are the fruits,*
*Take care of your garden*
*And keep out the weeds,*
*Fill it with sunshine,*
*Kind words and kind deeds.*

**—Henry Wadsworth Longfellow**

Grant me the ability to be alone.
May it be my custom to go outdoors each day
among the trees and grasses
among all growing things
and there may I be alone,
and enter into prayer
to talk with the one
that I belong to.

**—Rabbi Nachman of Bratzlav**

In gardens, beauty is a by-product. The main business is sex and death.

**—Sam Llewelyn**

❍❖❍

One should just sit quietly and look at a garden.
What you see depends on what you bring to it.

**—Sobin Yamada**

❍❖❍

Many things grow in the garden that were never sown there.

**—Thomas Fuller**

❍❖❍

- The garden is a mirror of the heart.
- The garden must be prepared in the soul first or else it will not flourish.

**—Anonymous**

# Tree Tales

Alone with myself
The trees bend to caress me
The shade hugs my heart.

**—Candy Polgar**

❍❖❍

High trees catch a lot of wind.

**—Dutch Proverb**

❍❖❍

To the great tree-loving fraternity we belong. We love trees with universal and unfeigned love, and all things that do grow under them or around them – the whole leaf and root tribe.

**—Henry Ward Beecher**

❍❖❍

If trees could scream, would we be so cavalier about cutting them down? We might, if they screamed all the time, for no good reason.

**—Jack Handey**

❍❖❍

*Against the earth's sweet flowing breast;*
*A tree that looks at God all day*
*And lifts her leafy arms to pray;*
*A tree that may in summer wear*
*A nest of robins in her hair;*
*Upon whose bosom snow has lain;*
*Who intimately lives with rain.*
*Poems are made by fools like me,*
*But only God can make a tree.*

**—Joyce Kilmer**

❍❖❍

*I think that I shall never see*
*A billboard lovely as a tree.*
*Perhaps, unless the billboards fall,*
*I'll never see a tree at all.*

**—Ogden Nash**

❍❖❍

God has cared for these trees, saved them from drought, disease, avalanches, and a thousand tempests and floods. But he cannot save them from fools.

**—John Muir**

❍❖❍

Trees are poems that earth writes upon the sky,
We fell them down and turn them into paper,
That we may record our emptiness.

**—Kahlil Gibran**

❍❖❍

*There is a pleasure in the pathless woods,*
*There is a rapture on the lonely shore,*
*There is society, where none intrudes,*
*By the deep sea, and music in its roar*
*I love not Man the less, but Nature more.*

**—Lord Byron**

❍❖❍

Who leaves the pine-tree, leaves his friend,
Unnerves his strength, invites his end.

**—Ralph Waldo Emerson**

❍❖❍

Save a tree. Eat a beaver.

**—Anonymous**

# Ant Antics

When the ants unite their mouths, they can carry an elephant.

**—Mossian Proverb**

❍❖❍

The greatest enemies of ants are other ants, just as the greatest enemies of men are other men.

**—Auguste Forel**

❍❖❍

If ants are such busy workers, how come they find the time to go to all the picnics?

**—Marie Dressler**

❍❖❍

Do not kill ants. They are your best friends.

**—Joe Brainard**

❍❖❍

An ant on the move does more than a dozing ox.

**—Lao Tzu**

❍❖❍

Only two great groups of animals, men and ants, indulge in highly organised mass warfare.

**—Charles H Maskins**

❍❖❍

Be thine enemy an ant; see in him an elephant.

**—Turkish Proverb**

# Man & Miscellany

Keep five yards from a carriage, ten yards from a horse, and a hundred yards from an elephant; but the distance one should keep from a wicked man cannot be measured.

**—Indian Proverb**

❍❖❍

The trouble with the rat race is that even if you win, you're still a rat.

**—Lily Tomlin**

❍❖❍

An appeaser is one who feeds a crocodile, hoping it will eat him last.

**—Winston Churchill**

❍❖❍

There are times when even the best manager is like the little boy with the big dog. Waiting to see where the dog wants to go so he can take him there.

**—Lee Iacocca**

❍❖❍

A traveller must have the back of an ass to bear all, a tongue like the tail of a dog to flatter all, the mouth of a hog to eat what is set before him, the ear of a merchant to hear all and say nothing.

**—Thomas Nashe**

❍❖❍

The circus is a place where horses, ponies and elephants are permitted to see men, women and children acting the fool.

**—Ambrose Bierce**

❍❖❍

My wings are a thousand books.

**—Gill Rob Wilson**

❍✣❍

*Let Hercules himself do what he may,*
*The cat will mew and the dog will have his day.*

**—William Shakespeare**

❍✣❍

There are joys which long to be ours. God sends ten thousands truths, which come about us like birds seeking inlet; but we are shut up to them, and so they bring us nothing, but sit and sing awhile upon the roof, and then fly away.

**—Henry Ward Beecher**

❍✣❍

The man who has to muck out the monkeys is rarely if ever consulted when the architects roll up in their limousines to sketch out the new monkey-house.

**—David Taylor**

❍✣❍

To me the most important thing is the sense of going on. You know how beautiful things are when you're travelling.

**—Edward Hopper**

❍✣❍

There is no beautifier of complexion or form or behaviour like the wish to scatter joy, and not pain, around us.

**—Emerson**

❍✣❍

For every beauty, there is an eye somewhere to see it.
For every truth, there is a ear somewhere to hear it.
For every love, there is a heart somewhere to receive it.

**—Ivan Panin**

❍✣❍

We live in a wonderful world that is full of beauty, charm and adventure. There is no end to the adventures that we can have if only we seek them with our eyes open.

**—Jawaharlal Nehru**

❍✣❍

The future belongs to those who believe in the beauty of their dreams.

**—Roosevelt**

❍❖❍

Many birds and beasts are... as fit to go to Heaven as many human beings – people who talk of their seats there with as much confidence as if they had booked them at a box-office.

**—Leigh Hunt**

❍❖❍

Hope is the thing with feathers that perches in the soul, and sings the tune without the words, and never stops at all.

**—Emily Dickinson**

❍❖❍

The worthiest people are the most injured by slander, as is the best fruit, which the birds have been pecking at.

**—Jonathan Swift**

❍❖❍

As the wandering sparrow, as the flying swallow, so the curse that is baseless shall not come home.

**—Proverb**

❍❖❍

I am beginning to learn that it is the sweet, simple things of life, which are the real ones after all.

**—Laura Ingalls Wilder**

❍❖❍

The love of wilderness is more than a hunger for what is always beyond our reach; it is also an expression of loyalty to the earth, the only home we shall ever know; the only paradise we ever need – if we only had the eyes to see.

**—Edward Abbey**

❍❖❍

We smile at the ignorance of the savage who cuts down the tree in order to reach its fruit; but the same blunder is made by every person who is over eager and impatient in the pursuit of pleasure.

**—William Ellery Channing**

❍❖❍

A man has to live with himself, and he should see to it that he always has good company.

**—Charles Evans Hughes**

❍❖❍

- We are all of us living in the gutter, but some of us are looking at the stars.
- Men become old, but they never become good.

**—Oscar Wilde**

❍❖❍

Tears are the summer showers to the soul.

**—Alfred Austin**

❍❖❍

A good cook is like a sorceress who dispenses happiness.

**—Elsa Schiaparelli**

❍❖❍

Laughter is the shortest distance between two people.

**—Victor Borge**

❍❖❍

Profanity is merely an expression of one's emotions.

**—Alanis Morrisette**

❍❖❍

Rituals are important. Nowadays it's hip not to be married. I'm not interested in being hip.

**—John Lennon**

❍❖❍

I think it's probably a good thing to be considered stable, but with a capacity for madness.

**—Wayne Coyne**

❍❖❍

Man comes naked into this world and again he departs naked. Such destiny shall attend him, as God's pen hath recorded upon his forehead.

**—Guru Nanak**

❍❖❍

In a way, I'd rather ride down the street on a camel than give what is sometimes called an in-depth interview. I'd rather ride down the street on a camel nude. In a snowstorm. Backwards.

**—Warren Beatty**

❍❖❍

Man invented language to satisfy his deep need to complain.

**—Lily Tomlin**

❍❖❍

If a man can write a better book, preach a better sermon, or make a better mouse-trap than his neighbour, though he builds his house in the woods, the world will make a beaten path to his door.

**—Ralph Waldo Emerson**

❍❖❍

As the monkey sacrifices its life at the feet of the hunter, so does a man at the feet of a beautiful woman.

**—Sri Ramakrishna**

❍❖❍

When men come to like a sea-life, they are not fit to live on land.

**—Samuel Johnson**

The capacity of human beings to bore one another seems to be vastly greater than that of any other animal.

**—HL Mencken**

❍❖❍

- We should be careful to get out of an experience only the wisdom that is in it – and stop there; lest we be like the cat that sits down on a hot stove-lid. She will never sit down on a hot stove-lid again, and that is well; but also, she will never sit down on a cold one anymore.
- Indecency, vulgarity, obscenity – these are strictly confined to man; he invented them. Among the higher animals there is no trace of them. They hide nothing. They are not ashamed.

**—Mark Twain**

Telling a teenager the facts of life is like giving a fish a bath.

**—Arnold Glasgow**

❍❖❍

Human beings lack the strength of the gorilla, the sharp teeth of the lion, the speed of the cheetah. Brainpower is our specialty.... With it we have developed machines that can lift more than many gorillas, knives that are sharper than any lion's teeth, and ways of travelling that make a cheetah's pace tediously slow. But the ability to reason is a peculiar ability. Unlike strong arms, sharp teeth or flashing legs, it can take us to conclusions we had no desire to reach.

**—Peter Singer**

- Beauty is potent, but money is omnipotent.
- A kind heart is a fountain of gladness, making everything in its vicinity freshen into smiles.
- Don't mind criticism. If it is untrue, disregard it; if unfair, keep from irritation; if it is ignorant, smile; if it is justified, it is not criticism, learn from it.
- If there is light in the soul,<br>there will be beauty in the person.<br>If there is beauty in the person,<br>there will be harmony in the house.<br>If there is harmony in the house,<br>there will be order in the nation.<br>If there is order in the nation,<br>there will be peace in the world.

**—Anonymous**

# Notable Quotes & Noble Thoughts

*—Shyamal Bhattacharjee*

***• Management • Politics***
***• Peace • War***

The book is written on certain practical real life incidents which took place when the author was a manager in the various industries that he had served. Life has become so complicated that in an attempt to rush and achieve success, human beings have become mechanical. Temper, anger, lust, jealousy, managerial gimmicks, warfare have become a fast living of the day. The fittest survives and the deserving one takes a back seat. Frustration has been a major disease for mankind.

This book is written especially for those who have forgotten what life is, in order to attain status, prestige, success, name and fame. A careful reading of the book will enable the readers about managing their life, and obtaining their end through peace. Quotes on politics and war add colour to the book and the readers will enjoy browsing through the pages to make their life meaningful and happy.

***Demy Size • Pages: 96***
***Price: Rs. 60/- • Postage: Rs. 15/-***